We make it easy!
2 CDs of dialogue,
sound effects, music

# instant Puppet skits

## Mikal Keefer & John Cutshall

## 20 Stories From People Who Met Jesus

# Group resources actually work!

This Group resource incorporates our R.E.A.L. approach to ministry. It reinforces a growing friendship with Jesus, encourages long-term learning, and results in life transformation, because it's

**Relational**
Learner-to-learner interaction enhances learning and builds Christian friendships.

**Experiential**
What learners experience through discussion and action sticks with them up to 9 times longer than what they simply hear or read.

**Applicable**
The aim of Christian education is to equip learners to be both hearers and doers of God's Word.

**Learner-based**
Learners understand and retain more when the learning process takes into consideration how they learn best.

## Dedications

To Jennifer, whose laugh is better than gold.
Always remember the Easter break when the puppets invaded.
—John Cutshall

For Adrienne, who'd rather have a good story than a good pizza any day.
—Mikal Keefer

**Instant Puppet Skits: 20 Stories From People Who Met Jesus**
Copyright © 2003 by John Cutshall and Mikal Keefer

Visit our website: **group.com**

**Credits**
Editor: Karl Leuthauser
Chief Creative Officer: Joani Schultz
Copy Editor: Lyndsay E. Gerwing
Art Director: Randy Kady
Print Production Artists: Shelly Dillon and Joyce Douglas
Cover Art Director: Bambi Eitel
Cover Designer: Blukazoo
Cover Photographer:Daniel Treat
Illustrator: Eldon Doty
Audio Producer: Jay Lowder
Production Manager: Peggy Naylor

Custom Puppets supplied for cover by:
One Way Street, Inc., P.O. Box 5077, Englewood, CO 80155-5077
303-790-1188. www.onewaystreet.com

Unless otherwise noted, Scripture taken from the HOLY BIBLE, NEW INTERNATIONAL VERSION®. Copyright © 1973, 1978, 1984 by International Bible Society. Used by permission of Zondervan Publishing House. All rights reserved.

**Library of Congress Cataloging-in-Publication Data**
Cutshall, John R. (John Robert), 1959-
Instant puppet skits : 20 stories from people who met Jesus / by John R. Cutshall and Mikal Keefer.
   p. cm.
ISBN 0-7644-2458-0 (pbk. : alk. paper)
1. Puppet theater in Christian education. I. Keefer, Mikal, 1954- II. Title.
BV1535.9.P8 C88 2002
246'.725--dc21
         2002011515

15 14 13 12 11      17 16 15 14 13 12
Printed in the United States of America.

# Contents

# Contents

# Welcome to the Show!

Want to see a child's eyes light up? Introduce the child to a puppet. Puppet shows are a surefire way to snag a child's attention. And that makes puppet shows a compelling way to introduce children to Bible stories and Bible characters.

The twenty scripts you'll find in *Instant Puppet Skits* have something in common: Each script tells the story of someone who had a personal encounter with Jesus. And you'll find that the scripts have other things in common too:

- Each script provides a way to involve the audience. Sometimes they'll have a part in the skit, and other times they'll provide a sound effect or a prop.

- After each script you'll find questions designed to help children apply what they've experienced and draw closer in their own relationships with Jesus.

- Scripts have no more than four puppets on stage at any one time, and often fewer. That makes it easy for you to recruit enough puppeteers!

- And each script is already recorded on a fun soundtrack. You and your puppeteer friends don't have to worry about digging up sound effects or reading the lines as you perform. It's already done for you!

# How to Perform a Puppet Skit

## 1. Recruit puppeteers

Involve children every chance you have! Maybe your performance production values will suffer, but the learning your children experience more than makes up for the occasional missed exits and entrances.

## 2. Create a stage

You can get by with a table turned on its side, but you'll be more comfortable and provide better performances if you design a puppet stage that includes these elements:

- an elevated stage area,

- side panels,

- lighting controls (so you can dim the stage lights), and

- a backstage pad to save wear and tear on your puppeteers' knees.

### 3. Select a skit

Listen to the CD and then assign roles to specific puppets and puppeteers. In the table of contents of this book, you'll also find Scripture references for each skit to help you select which skits will fit into your upcoming programs.

### 4. Collect props and build sets

These skits are intentionally prop and set "light," so you'll need very few items. To give your puppets a Bible-times appearance, you will want to create simple robes sized to the puppets you'll use in these skits.

### 5. Practice, practice, practice

See "A Puppet Primer" (p. 7) for a short list of skills you'll want your puppeteers to master. Also make certain puppeteers are familiar with specific scripts before performing them—including lines, emotions, blocking, and entrances and exits.

### 6. Break a leg!

Perform your show! Use the prerecorded soundtrack, or work without it—it's your choice!

# Staging Terms

We use simple stage instructions to help you move the puppets. You'll want everyone on your team to know these terms so that, during rehearsals, it's easy to communicate where you want puppets to move.

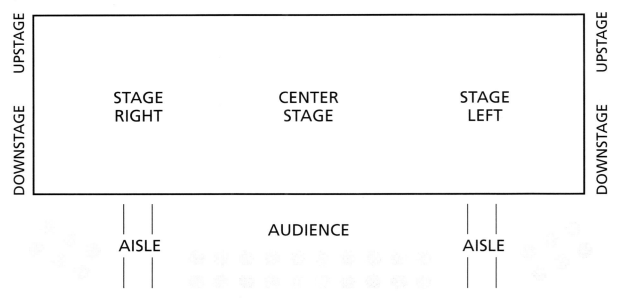

**STAGE TERMS**

# How to Create Simple Bible-Times Costumes

Use the simple illustrations below to help you create inexpensive cape-robes for your puppets. Because puppets come in so many different sizes, we haven't attempted to provide measurements. You'll need to tailor a robe for puppets you want to use in these skits.

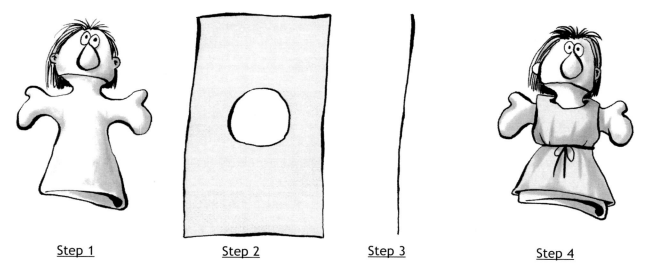

Step 1          Step 2          Step 3          Step 4

# A Puppet Primer

The best thing about working with puppets is that puppets grab children's imaginations. When you're leading a puppet show, you aren't just sending your puppets scampering across a makeshift stage in the corner of your room. You're also playing on the grand stage of your children's imaginations.

With a twist of your wrist, you can convince children that a large, talking, purple dog has hit a home run. Your nimble fingers can send a marionette tap-dancing across a fairy-tale carpet of flowers. Lowering a simple yellow disk on a stick to show the sun setting can be enough to cause droopy eyes.

A good puppet show connects with kids in a way that's powerful and effective, so you want to do it well.

Whether you're a solo artist who's just beginning or you direct a team of experienced puppeteers, there are disciplines you'll want to master. Why? Any puppeteer who has dropped a prop or forgotten to come in on cue knows how fast a group of children will zero in on a mistake. Those distractions take away from the fun, the imagination, and, most important, the message.

To keep children focused on the message, practice the following skills until your puppets shine.

## Lip-sync with precision.

If you're using puppets with moving mouths, be careful to minimize the amount of mouth movement. When people speak, it's primarily the lower jaw that moves. When your puppets speak, simulate the same movement. Use your thumb to move the lower jaw of your puppet, and don't open the mouth wide unless you want your puppet to show surprise.

## Improve puppet posture.

Puppeteering is hard work! It's tempting to relax a bit by letting your arm drift down, especially if you're working behind an elevated stage and you have to keep your arms above your head.

Always keep your arms at a 90-degree angle to the floor. The characters you're portraying wouldn't walk leaning over, so don't let them. Some puppeteers use a slight bobbing motion to simulate running when puppets dash from one place to another. It's a good technique, but if you use it, be sure *everyone* in your puppet troupe uses it for consistency's sake.

One thing to keep in mind if you're developing a puppet troupe: The puppeteers must have the upper body strength to keep puppets upright.

## Look directly at your audience.

These scripts call for occasionally addressing your audience directly. When you do so, be sure to make direct "eye contact" by having your puppets "look" directly at the children. If children are seated on the floor, or your stage is high, make the appropriate adjustment by angling your wrists.

## Know what's in view.

Raise your arm too high and it's painfully obvious that Zacchaeus doesn't have feet—he's walking around on a forearm. Not good.

Practice makes perfect. And if you're able, consider having a monitor hooked up to an inconspicuous video camera that's out in front of the stage. Place the monitor where your puppeteers can see it as they perform. But be careful; this technique may be distracting and create more problems than it solves.

## Be able to make a graceful entrance and exit.

When making entrances and exits, be consistent about whether you let puppets "stair-step" (move up and down as if climbing or descending steps) at the edge of the stage or whether they'll move off stage fully standing.

An easy way to resolve the situation is to build a stage that features side panels with ample room for puppeteers to move puppets out of sight before dropping them below the audience's sightline.

## Know your script.

Certain Shakespearean actors might disagree, but we think puppet plays may be more challenging than people plays, and here's why:

Puppets can't read the audience. When you're doubled over with both arms high over your head, wondering how you'll sneak past another puppeteer so your puppets can cross the stage and exit, you can't see how the audience is responding. You have to rely just on what you hear. When the audience unexpectedly laughs, it may be because you were brilliant delivering a line...or because a puppet's head just fell off.

Having whatever script you're using down cold lets you pay attention to the details that can turn a good performance into a great one.

Know the lines. Know the blocking. Practice stage movement.

# Trim Your Cast—and Cut Costs

Something you'll quickly discover about puppets: They can be pricey. Even when you create your own, you'll find that they're expensive to make and maintain.

Here's a way to trim the number of puppets you'll need for these skits: Create an *ensemble cast*. That is, always use one puppet to play the part of a bumbling sidekick, another to be the female lead, and another to play the director or hero.

Creating an ensemble cast is a strategy that has served Jim Henson Productions and the Muppets well.

Think about it: Kermit the Frog plays many different roles throughout the Muppet movies and television programs, but he's always essentially the same character: the reasonable, calm, "Everyman" who finds himself surrounded with more colorful characters. Miss Piggy is always the self-possessed prima donna, and Fozzie is always the scattered, hyper, kindhearted sideman.

We've provided a recommended cast list for you to use if you want to keep your puppets' characters consistent as you present these scripts. Doing so lets you do all these scripts with just a few puppets and two socks.

The four primary puppet characters you'll need if you create an ensemble include:

**NORTON** is a levelheaded character who doesn't panic, even in the midst of chaos. He's the perfect narrator or leader, though he's not used to anyone in the ensemble cast actually following him.

**NORTON**

**EDWARD** has played Macbeth and is a serious thespian. He regards himself a bit above the novices he has been reduced to acting alongside, but the show must go on. Prone to occasional tantrums, he has been known to sulk in his dressing room. He's capable of brilliance on stage, but not as often as he imagines.

**EDWARD**

**SUE** is a strong, caring character who is self-aware and able to speak with certainty. Her melodic voice makes her a great narrator. She's steady and aware, a character who moves with purpose and conviction.

**SUE**

**FRITZ** is easily excited and eager to please, but he seldom has a complete grasp on what's happening around him. He tends to move about quickly and is perfect as comic relief.

**FRITZ**

If you create an ensemble, here's how they can fit with the skits in this book:

## The Christmas Miracle
Director: Sue
Actor: Edward
Shepherd Boy 1: Any puppet
Shepherd Boy 2: Any puppet

## Teacher at the Temple
Rabbi Rosen: Edward
Host: Norton
Associate Producer: Fritz

## John the Baptist
Host: Edward
John the Baptist: Norton

## Apostle Andrew
Fisherman: Fritz
Apostle Andrew: Edward

## Planning the Wedding
Caterer: Norton
Assistant Caterer: Fritz

## Friend of the Paralytic
Elias: Edward
Friend: Fritz

## Clear the Temple
Tourist: Norton
Construction Worker: Fritz
Joe: Edward

## Nicodemus
Man: Norton
Nicodemus: Edward

## Centurion and Servant
Centurion: Norton
Servant: Fritz

## Fish and Loaves
Hot Dog Salesman: Edward
Boy: Fritz

## Peter on the Water
Disciple 1: Norton
Disciple 2: Fritz
Peter: Edward

## Grateful Leper
Doctor: Norton
David: Fritz

## Mary and Martha
Mary: Sue
Mike Rophone: Norton

## Lazarus
Bernie: Fritz
Lazarus: Norton

## Prodigal Son
Director: Norton
Bruce: Edward
Daphne: Sue
Frankie: Fritz

## Little Girl on His Lap
Disciple 7: Edward
Father 1: Norton
Father 2: Fritz
Little Girl: Sue

## Zacchaeus
Man: Norton
EMT 1: Towel
EMT 2: Towel
Zacchaeus: Fritz

## The Last Supper
Jim: Edward
Ruth: Sue

## The Centurion and the Soldier
Roman Centurion: Norton
Soldier: Edward

## Mary Magdalene
Mary Magdalene: Sue
Peter: Norton
John: Edward

# The Christmas Miracle

**Bible Reference:** Luke 2:8-18

## Cast

**DIRECTOR:** tired, overwhelmed woman who is struggling to stay even-tempered

**ACTOR:** dramatic, pompous, and definitely difficult artist

**SHEPHERD BOY 1:** innocent and wide-eyed boy

**SHEPHERD BOY 2:** tired and cranky boy

**VOICE:** offstage production helper

## Costuming: All characters wear Bible-times costumes.

## Props: Bible-times costumes, a small script taped to Director's hand, and a sign that reads:

> Coming Soon:
> *The Christmas Miracle*
> A Play in Three Acts

## Setup: Before the skit begins, seat four or five trusted children down front and center. Give each of these children a flashlight, and appoint them the Spotlight Crew. When instructed, they'll turn on their flashlights and shine them as directed. When asked to turn off the flashlights, they'll do so.

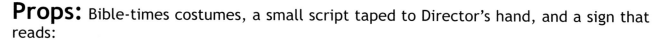

| ACTIONS | WORDS |
|---|---|
|  *Play track 1 on CD A.* | |
| DIRECTOR enters from STAGE LEFT and then looks left and right while giving directions. | |
| DIRECTOR calls OFFSTAGE RIGHT. | **DIRECTOR** <br> **(Calling)** Places everyone! Places! You there, shepherd! Do something with those sheep; they're eating the carpet! <br><br> Spotlight Crew, hit me with the lights, and let's see if they're working...OK, that's good, focus on me. OK, turn 'em off. |

Look, people, *The Christmas Miracle* opens in four days. That's *four days,* people, and we are *not* ready. Let's make this rehearsal count! Everyone, take your places and let's go. Act One again...this time without dropping the star through the roof of the stable, OK?

ACTOR enters from STAGE RIGHT.

**ACTOR**
(**Indignant**) Director, we *must* talk...

DIRECTOR stops what he is doing and looks at ACTOR.

**DIRECTOR**
(**Long-suffering**) What now?

ACTOR moves dramatically as he talks with DIRECTOR.

**ACTOR**
(**Indignant**) I must protest madame! You have me playing the part of a common innkeeper, but I am an *actor,* madame. I have played *Shakespeare,* madame. *Hamlet!*

**DIRECTOR**
(**Struggling to stay patient**) Look, Hamlet isn't in this play. You're an innkeeper. You're supposed to be over by the inn. You know, so Mary and Joseph can come over and you can send them out to the stable.

ACTOR continues dramatically.

**ACTOR**
(**Indignant**) There it *is*! That's the *problem*! You've cast me in the role of a *villain*! What kind of person would send a woman to a stable to have her baby?

DIRECTOR looks down as if checking notes and looks at ACTOR.

**DIRECTOR**
You. You're that kind of person. It's right here in the script.

ACTOR throws up hands.

**ACTOR**
But what's my *motivation*?

**Skit One:**
The Christmas Miracle

**DIRECTOR**
There's no room in the inn. See here on page 47? You say, "There is no room in the inn."

ACTOR continues his dramatics.

**ACTOR**
I have *fans*, madame! Boys and girls who look to me as their *hero*! A hero would *never* turn away Mary and Joseph! Have one of those *shepherds* say there's no room in the inn.

DIRECTOR gently shakes his head.

**DIRECTOR**
They can't. They're out tending their flocks by night. It's up to you.

ACTOR throws up his hands and turns his back to DIRECTOR.

**ACTOR**
*Outrageous*, madame! I *demand* you change the script!

**DIRECTOR**
(Growing impatient) I *can't* change the script! It's in the Bible! That's how it happened: Mary and Joseph came to Bethlehem, the inn was full, and you sent them back to a stable where Mary gave birth to Jesus.

ACTOR doesn't turn around.

**ACTOR**
But I *insist*...

DIRECTOR shakes with frustration.

**DIRECTOR**
(Exasperated) No can do! Forget it! Over and out! No changes!

ACTOR turns to face DIRECTOR, delivers his line, then turns to exit STAGE RIGHT.

**ACTOR**
Madame, I shall be in my dressing room until you come to your senses and *apologize*!

ACTOR exits as DIRECTOR speaks.

**DIRECTOR**
(Calling) You don't *have* a dressing room!

| | |
|---|---|
| | **Actor**<br>(**Calling back**) Then I'll be in *your* dressing room! |
| | **DIRECTOR**<br>(**Calling**) I don't have a dressing room either! |
| DIRECTOR looks at audience and slumps as if discouraged. | (**Sighs**) |
| | **ACTOR**<br>Then I'll...I'll just shut myself in this trunk and stay here until you apologize! |
| | There! *Now* you'll be sorry! |
| | **DIRECTOR**<br>(**Sighs**) This Christmas the *miracle* will be if we get through this rehearsal... |
| DIRECTOR looks STAGE RIGHT. | (**Calling**) Hey, I said the shepherds would be watching their *flocks* by night, not washing their *socks* by night! Enough with the laundry! |
| | **VOICE**<br>Sorry! |
| DIRECTOR slumps even lower. | **DIRECTOR**<br>(**Sighs**) |
| SHEPHERD BOY 1 walks on from STAGE LEFT. | **SHEPHERD BOY 1**<br>Hey, miss? |
| DIRECTOR looks at SHEPHERD BOY 1. | **DIRECTOR**<br>Look, you're the shepherd boy, right? If the sheep are still hungry, feed them the seat cushions... |
| SHEPHERD BOY 1 looks right at DIRECTOR. | **SHEPHERD BOY 1**<br>(**Innocently wide-eyed and excited**) I wanted to tell someone—I just saw Jesus! |

**Skit One:**
*The Christmas Miracle*

Over there in that stable. He was wrapped in swaddling clothes and lying in a manger.

DIRECTOR looks to ceiling in relief.

**DIRECTOR**
Glad to hear that at least *someone* knows the story. And great job with the costume. You might want to wash it now and then, though. You smell like a real shepherd boy.

ACTOR calls from OFFSTAGE.

**ACTOR**
(Calling) I'm waiting for that apology!

**SHEPHERD BOY 1**
(Still excited and innocent) And you know what was amazing? He's just a baby, a couple hours old, but *already* Jesus is a King!

DIRECTOR nods his head "yes."

**DIRECTOR**
Well, sure. Jesus is the Son of God. He's the *King* of kings.

SHEPHERD BOY 1 points OFFSTAGE LEFT.

**SHEPHERD BOY 1**
Out in the fields when the angels appeared, I thought *that* was something! But then we came into town to look for the new King. There was this star...

DIRECTOR nods his head "yes."

**DIRECTOR**
Yeah, I know...stuck in the roof of the stable. We'll get that fixed.

**SHEPHERD BOY 1**
We found the stable, we walked in, and we bowed. None of us had ever seen a real king before. We didn't know what to say. We didn't have any gifts, or good clothes to wear, or anything. We were sort of afraid.

| | |
|---|---|
| DIRECTOR looks down at script. | **DIRECTOR**<br>You know, this is good stuff! Add this to your lines. |
| | **SHEPHERD BOY 1**<br>But it didn't matter! Mary and Joseph let us come right up to the manger so we could peek inside. Jesus was sleeping, but I think he knew we were there anyway. I could *feel* it. |
| DIRECTOR nods in agreement. | **DIRECTOR**<br>Kid, I'm adding all this to page 53. Say it just that way. |
| ACTOR calls from OFFSTAGE. | **ACTOR**<br>(Calling) I'm not kidding—I want that apology! |
| SHEPHERD BOY 1 exits STAGE LEFT. | **SHEPHERD BOY 1**<br>Look, Miss, I'd like to stay and talk, but I've got to go tell people what I saw! I've just seen *Jesus*! I've seen the Son of God! |
| DIRECTOR calls to OFFSTAGE LEFT. | **DIRECTOR**<br>(Calling) Hey, where are you going? Shepherd boy! Hey, shepherd boy! |
| SHEPHERD BOY 2 enters STAGE RIGHT. | **SHEPHERD BOY 2**<br>Whataya want? |
| DIRECTOR looks around SHEPHERD BOY 2. | **DIRECTOR**<br>I want the shepherd boy to get back here. |
| SHEPHERD BOY 2 shakes his head. | **SHEPHERD BOY 2**<br>First you want me over *there* rounding up sheep, then you want me over *here*. Make up your mind. |

**Skit One:**
The Christmas Miracle

**DIRECTOR**
(Astounded) You...*you're* our shepherd boy?

SHEPHERD BOY nods his head "yes."

**SHEPHERD BOY 2**
Yup. I wanted to be Joseph, but you said I was too short.

DIRECTOR looks STAGE LEFT.

**DIRECTOR**
Then who was *that*?

SHEPHERD BOY 2 looks around.

**SHEPHERD BOY 2**
Who was *who*? I didn't see anybody.

**DIRECTOR**
(Astounded) That shepherd boy who just left. The one who smelled so *real*.

SHEPHERD BOY 2 brings one hand to chest.

**SHEPHERD BOY 2**
*I'm* the only shepherd boy in this play as far as I know, and right now *I* don't have any sheep.

**DIRECTOR**
(Distracted) Well, go get them corralled or rounded up or something.

**SHEPHERD BOY 2**
Sheesh! Directors!

SHEPHERD BOY 2 exits STAGE RIGHT.

ACTOR calls from OFFSTAGE.

**ACTOR**
(Calling) I haven't heard an *apology* yet...

**DIRECTOR**
(Awestruck) Wow...I think I know what our Christmas Miracle is...

DIRECTOR exits STAGE RIGHT.

**ACTOR**
OK, I guess you've learned your lesson. I'll come out now...(thump)

Umm...*Now* I'll come out...

Um...Would anyone out there have a hammer?

Hello? Anyone there? Anyone?

## For Deeper Learning

Say: **We can't really talk with the shepherds who met Jesus on the first Christmas night. But we *can* know and love Jesus ourselves!**

Have children form groups of three or four and discuss:

- **How do you think the shepherds who went to see and worship Jesus felt when they got to the stable? Why?**

- **If you could see Jesus face to face, what would you say? What would you do? Why?**

- **If you love and follow Jesus, you'll see him in heaven. How will you feel then?**

**Skit One:**
The Christmas Miracle

# Teacher at the Temple

**Bible Reference:** Luke 2:41-52

## Cast

**RABBI ROSEN:** elderly, prickly Jewish gentleman

**HOST:** male adult who is trying to stay calm as his show collapses around him

**FRITZ THE ASSOCIATE PRODUCER:** adult male who is a bit rough around the edges and not terribly bright

## Costuming: All puppets should be in Bible-times costumes.

## Props: Bible-times costumes and a sign that reads, "Important People in History"

## Setup: Place the sign at stage left.

---

SCRIPT

| ACTIONS | WORDS |
|---|---|
|  *Play track 2 on CD A.*<br><br>HOST enters from STAGE RIGHT and crosses to CENTER STAGE. | **HOST**<br>Ladies and gentlemen, welcome to our television show, "Important People in History." I'm Norton, your host. Each week an important person in history shows up, and we ask the person some questions. We'll begin filming in a few moments, but first I want to remind you to applaud when our guest comes on stage so he feels welcome.<br><br>While we're waiting, I'd like to know what famous people you'd like to meet. Turn to a neighbor, and tell that person the name of an actor or music star you'd like us to invite to our show. You have fifteen seconds. Go ahead; I can wait. Talk to the person sitting next to you.<br><br>**(15 SECONDS)** Dum, de dum, ta-dah-dum-dum... |

OK, everyone shout out the names of famous people you want to meet. Let's hear it. All at once, please—shout out names.

Uh, huh...yeah...sure. OK, got it.

I'll see what we can do. But now I'd like to introduce you to a famous teacher from the Temple University and a man who was *my* teacher when I was in school. Ladies and gentlemen, put your hands together and let's give a warm welcome to Rabbi Rosen!

I said, *Rabbi Rosen*!

HOST turns to STAGE LEFT.

HOST waits for four seconds—nothing happens.

FRITZ sticks his head onto stage from STAGE RIGHT.

HOST goes to FRITZ.

**FRITZ**
(Stage whisper) Pssst! Hey, Norton! Come here!

**HOST**
Excuse me, ladies and gentlemen. Must be a little glitch...

So what's up?

**FRITZ**
(Stage whisper) The Rabbi ain't here!

**HOST**
(Stage whisper, disbelieving) What do you mean he's not here? I saw him here half an hour ago!

HOST looks at wrist as if checking his watch.

**FRITZ**
(Stage whisper) I mean he *ain't here.*

FRITZ raises his hands for emphasis.

**HOST**
(Stage whisper) Did you check the dressing room?

| | |
|---|---|
| FRITZ nods his head "yes." | **FRITZ**<br>(Stage whisper) There, the parking lot, the bathroom, the basement, *everywhere*! |
| HOST points OFFSTAGE. | **HOST**<br>(Stage whisper) Well, he has to be *somewhere*. Go find him! I'll stay here and stall... |
| | **FRITZ**<br>(Stage whisper) Got it, chief! I won't let you down! I'm on it! One rabbi comin' up! |
| FRITZ exits STAGE RIGHT; HOST crosses back to CENTER STAGE.<br><br>HOST turns to face audience. | **HOST**<br>Um, we seem to have a bit of a delay, ladies and gentlemen... |
| FRITZ calls OFFSTAGE. | **FRITZ**<br>(Calling) Oh, Rabbi...come out, come out wherever you are. |
| | **HOST**<br>I'm sure our guest will join us shortly, but while we're waiting... |
| FRITZ from OFFSTAGE. | **FRITZ**<br>Maybe he's in this closet...<br><br>Nope, not in *there*... |
| | **HOST**<br>Like I was saying, while we're waiting, I'll entertain us by telling a few jokes. Two puppets were in a rowboat, and the first puppet turned to the second puppet and said... |
| FRITZ is still OFFSTAGE. | **FRITZ**<br>Maybe he's in *this* closet...<br><br>Aaaahh! Nope, not *there*! |

**HOST**
And the second puppet said, "Hey, I see you have a parrot on your shoulder..."

RABBI enters from STAGE LEFT.

**RABBI**
Who's making all that racket? And you call that a joke?

HOST turns to face RABBI.

**HOST**
Rabbi! We thought you were lost!

RABBI dismisses the thought with a wave of his hand.

**RABBI**
Lost, schmost. I was getting a snack. So let's get started already.

HOST turns to audience.

**HOST**
(To audience) Ladies and gentlemen, this is Rabbi Rosen, my very favorite teacher.

RABBI looks HOST up and down in examination.

**RABBI**
I remember you—always turning things in late. But I taught at the Temple for more years than I can remember and I've had some bright students. *Wonderful* students.

**HOST**
Like me?

RABBI shakes his head "no."

**RABBI**
(Flatly) No. Not like you. Like Jesus.

**HOST**
(Surprised) You taught Jesus?

RABBI lifts his head in thought.

**RABBI**
Just for a few days, when he was twelve years old. Very polite. *Extremely* well studied. His mother and father had brought him to Jerusalem for the Passover, and he stopped by the Temple.

RABBI looks at HOST.

**HOST**

Did he sign up for your class?

**RABBI**

That young man could have *taught* my class. He came in, he listened to me and some of the other teachers, and then he started asking questions. *Great* questions, not at all like the kind of questions *you* used to ask.

**HOST**

You can remember what I asked after all these years? I'm flattered.

RABBI shakes his head in disappointment and looks up at ceiling.

**RABBI**

Don't be. You're the only student I've ever had who *every day* asked where to find the bathroom. *Aye, aye, aye.* The questions *Jesus* asked showed how much he understood. And when we asked *him* questions, it was like we were talking with another *teacher*. He was *amazing*!

Anyway, I found out that Jesus' parents didn't know he was at the Temple. They'd started home after the Passover and thought he was in the crowd. When they found him, they were plenty relieved, I'll tell you.

**HOST**

What did they say?

**RABBI**

Jesus said something remarkable. He told his mother, "Why were you searching for me? Didn't you know I had to be in my Father's house?" Jesus knew that *God* was his Father. A truly remarkable boy, that Jesus.

**HOST**

Rabbi Rosen, thanks for coming. One more question. You've won dozens of awards for excellent teaching. Which award are you proudest of?

RABBI raises his hand in testimony.

**RABBI**

That's easy: none of them. The thing I'm proudest of as a teacher is that for at least a few days, I was with Jesus. *That* is the shining moment.

**HOST**

Again, Rabbi, thanks for being here.

**RABBI**

You're welcome. And don't think I forgot that you owe me a term paper. You never turned it in.

HOST turns to audience.

**HOST**

Umm. That's the show for today, folks. Thanks for tuning in.

**RABBI**

(Calling) Don't think I'm *gonna* forget it, either. Ten pages! And watch your spelling!

RABBI slowly exiting STAGE LEFT.

HOST looks around nervously and exits STAGE RIGHT.

## For Deeper Learning

Say: **Jesus knew he was God's Son, and he wanted to know God. The Temple teachers were amazed at all Jesus knew and understood.**

**We can get to know God better, too.**

Have children form groups of three or four and discuss:

- **What's a way that we can get to know God better?**
- **What's something you know about God that amazes you?**
- **What's the one thing you'd like to tell your friends and family about God?**

# John the Baptist

**Bible Reference:** John 3:27-35

**Cast**

> **HOST:** self-absorbed adult emcee
> **JOHN:** humble and direct adult male

**Costuming:** Dress Host in a suit or normal clothing and John in Bible-times costume.

**Props:** Suit and Bible-times costume

---

## SCRIPT

| ACTIONS | WORDS |
|---|---|
|  *Play track 3 on CD A.*<br><br>HOST enters from STAGE LEFT and crosses to CENTER STAGE. | **HOST**<br>The management and actors wish to thank you for coming to our show. Before we start, I'm wondering if any of you happen to have a grasshopper on you. Would you check your pockets, please? **(3 second pause)**<br><br>Maybe on the bottom of your shoes? Anybody? Check, please. **(3 second pause)**<br><br>Oh, well. You see, today's special guest is really fond of grasshoppers. He eats them for lunch. And breakfast. *And* dinner.<br><br>We promised to have a snack for our guest, but that's before we discovered that a bowl of candy and a couple of root beers wouldn't do it. Look, would you at least help me make a grasshopper sound so he feels at home? I'll show you how it goes... |
| Calling OFFSTAGE RIGHT. | Fritz, roll the grasshopper tape! |

**FRITZ**
OK! Rolling tape!

**HOST**
That's it. Simplicity itself. Now please join me in trying it. Chirp along with the tape while Fritz plays it again three times.

Very good, but let's try it again louder. And this time everyone please join in.

JOHN enters from stage LEFT.

**JOHN**
(Brightly) Sounds like lunch!

HOST watches JOHN enter.

**HOST**
(Grandly) Ah, ladies and gentlemen, join me in greeting our special guest, John the Baptist.

JOHN crosses to CENTER STAGE and joins HOST during applause.

**JOHN**
(Curious) What's happening here?

HOST looks at JOHN.

**HOST**
We were waiting to meet you. I hoped you'd have a few words for the children.

JOHN turns to audience and opens his mouth as if to speak.

**JOHN**
(Nicely) Sure. Here's what I have to say...

HOST moves slightly between JOHN and audience.

**HOST**
(Cutting in) But before you speak, I've prepared a brief introduction.

JOHN closes his mouth and turns to HOST.

**JOHN**
I don't really need one...

HOST ignores JOHN and speaks to audience.

**HOST**
Guests, we are fortunate to have with us one of the greatest preachers of all time, a prince of the pulpit, a titan of teaching, a giant among men...

| | |
|---|---|
| JOHN looks at HOST. | **JOHN**<br>Thanks, but really... |
| HOST looks to audience. | **HOST**<br>And not only is John the Baptist... |
| HOST turns to JOHN. | May I call you John the Baptist? |
| | **JOHN**<br>Actually, I'd rather... |
| HOST ignores JOHN and talks to audience. | **HOST**<br>(**Self-importantly**) Not only is John the Baptist a master of the message, a teller of truth, a man who deserves our utmost respect, attention, and admiration, but he is *also* the cousin of Jesus. |
| | **JOHN**<br>Speaking of Jesus... |
| HOST making grand motions with his arms and head. | **HOST**<br>(**Grandly**) So it is with great pleasure that I welcome to our stage today this paragon of virtue, a man for this moment, none other than John the Baptist! Listen carefully—this is a historic moment you will remember forever! What message do you have for us today, John the Baptist? |
| JOHN turns from HOST to audience. | **JOHN**<br>(**Clears throat**) Ahem...repent. |
| | (**5 second pause**) |
| HOST looks from JOHN to audience and back to JOHN with a blank stare. | **HOST**<br>And? |
| JOHN looks to the HOST. | **JOHN**<br>That's all. Repent. Turn away from sin. |

HOST looks JOHN straight in the eye.

**HOST**
(**Protesting**) There must be *something* else.

JOHN looks up as if he were thinking.

**JOHN**
Oh, you're right! I almost forgot. Get to know Jesus.

**(4 second pause)**

HOST continues to look at JOHN.

**HOST**
(**Miffed**) I give you an introduction that took me four hours to write and all you have to say is "Repent. Get to know Jesus"?

JOHN nods his head in agreement.

**JOHN**
Um, yeah. That's my job: to point people to Jesus.

HOST looks at JOHN in disbelief.

**HOST**
(**Protesting**) But you yourself are famous!

**JOHN**
(**Kindly**) *Was* famous. Lately all my disciples have been heading over to join Jesus and travel with him.

**HOST**
Doesn't that bother you?

JOHN shakes his head "no."

**JOHN**
(**Cheerful**) Not at all. *He's* the Son of God. I'm just here to point people in his direction.

HOST shakes his head in disbelief.

**HOST**
(**Incredulous**) What about your preaching? Crowds used to come to the Jordan River to hear you speak. Hundreds of people. *Thousands* of people!

JOHN looks around as if letting HOST in on a big secret.

**JOHN**
**(Cheerful)** Lately it's been pretty much me and the grasshoppers. Hardly anybody shows up. They're all off listening to Jesus.

HOST looks around to see what JOHN is looking at and then back to JOHN.

**HOST**
So you're a...a *has-been*? You're a *failure*?

JOHN turns to audience.

**JOHN**
**(Kindly)** A failure? Me? No, not at all! I'm doing the most important thing I could *ever* do!

You see, *Jesus* is the light of the world, not me. Helping people meet Jesus is the most important thing I could ever do.

**HOST**
**(Disgusted)** Well, that's just *perfect*. Four hours writing an introduction! Two *days* looking for grasshoppers! This has been a complete waste of time! I'm going to be in my dressing room!

HOST storms off STAGE LEFT. JOHN watches him go.

**JOHN**
**(To self)** Guess he won't be inviting me back for another show. Oh, well.

JOHN turns to audience.

I'm going back to tell some more people about Jesus. If you don't know him yet, make sure you ask one of the adults here about Jesus today. 'Bye!

JOHN exits STAGE RIGHT

**Skit Three:**
*John the Baptist*

## For Deeper Learning

Say: Most people want to be as famous as they can be. We're like that, too, aren't we? We want people to notice us, admire us, like us, and think we're great!

But John the Baptist knew that Jesus was the most important person anyone could ever know, so John wanted people who came to see him to go see Jesus. John the Baptist pointed people to Jesus.

Have children form groups of three or four and discuss:

- Who's the most famous person you've ever seen in person? How did that feel?

- What would you have thought if the famous person you saw said, "Forget me; go meet Jesus"?

- In what ways can you point people to Jesus?

# Apostle Andrew

**Bible Reference:** Matthew 4:18-22

## Cast

**FISHERMAN:** young man with more enthusiasm than common sense

**APOSTLE ANDREW:** elderly man who is gentle but willing to confront

## Costuming: Dress Fisherman and Andrew in Bible-times costumes.

## Props: Bible-times costumes, small fishing pole or dowel rod

---

### SCRIPT

| ACTIONS | WORDS |
|---|---|
|  *Play track 4 on CD A.* | |
| FISHERMAN is at CENTER STAGE holding a fishing pole. He faces STAGE LEFT. | **FISHERMAN**<br>What a great day for fishing! Blue sky, sparkling water, the smell of old seaweed floating around...it's *perfect*! |
| ANDREW enters from STAGE RIGHT and crosses to CENTER STAGE. | **ANDREW**<br>Whatcha doin', young feller? |
| FISHERMAN makes a casting motion with his rod toward STAGE RIGHT. | **FISHERMAN**<br>Fishing! You may think all it takes is throwing a line in the water, but that's just the start. Fishing takes *brains*. It takes *skill*. It takes *accuracy*. |
| | **MAN**<br>(Offstage) Hey, watch where you throw that thing! |
| FISHERMAN shouts to MAN OFFSTAGE and then turns to ANDREW. | **FISHERMAN**<br>(Shouting) Sorry about that!<br><br>(To Andrew) Still working on the accuracy. |

| | |
|---|---|
| ANDREW looks at FISHERMAN. | **ANDREW**<br>Years ago I did a bit of fishing myself. Did it for a livin' for a long time... |
| FISHERMAN looks over the audience as if dreaming. | **FISHERMAN**<br>Me, I *love* fishing. The fresh air, the thrill of the chase, reelin' in the big ones. |
| ANDREW matches FISHERMAN'S pose as if he, too, were dreaming. | **ANDREW**<br>Yeah, I know what you mean. But I couldn't help but notice that you fish a bit different than everyone else. |
| FISHERMAN breaks out of the dream and looks at ANDREW. | **FISHERMAN**<br>What do you mean? |
| ANDREW points to audience. | **ANDREW**<br>Well, the water is over *there*...<br><br>See all those fish? They're wiggling their tails. Wiggle your tails, fish! And they're opening and closing their mouths wide. Do that, you fish! And they're moving their fins back and forth. Let's see some fins move, fish! Thanks, fish. You can just sit still in the water again. **(To Fisherman)** And you seem to be fishing over *here*, on the land. |
| ANDREW points to FISHERMAN. | And I was lookin' at what you're using for bait. What *is* that? |
| FISHERMAN casts again. | **FISHERMAN**<br>PB&T. |
| FISHERMAN looks at where he has cast his line. | **ANDREW**<br>PB&T? |
| ANDREW looks at FISHERMAN in amazement. | **FISHERMAN**<br>Peanut butter and tuna fish. On rye. Earlier today I was using lollipops and yo-yos. |
| FISHERMAN nods his head "yes." | |

**Skit Four:**
*Apostle Andrew*

ANDREW slowly shakes his head left to right to show his disbelief.

**ANDREW**
Son, I've been fishing longer than you've been alive, and I've *never* heard of using yo-yos for bait. What kind of fish are you *after*?

FISHERMAN continues to look out at his line.

**FISHERMAN**
I'm after the biggest, sneakiest, hardest-headed thing on this planet...

ANDREW looks where FISHERMAN is looking.

**ANDREW**
The Polka-Dotted Sea Bass?

FISHERMAN shakes his head "no."

**FISHERMAN**
(Dismissively) No, *way* too easy!

**ANDREW**
The Undergirted Gar-Blower?

ANDREW looks at audience and then up in the air as if he's thinking.

**FISHERMAN**
Naw...got one of those last year. Tastes like chicken.

ANDREW looks at FISHERMAN.

**ANDREW**
Then you must be after the Shovel-Faced Bluntnose! They're mean and ugly, and you might want to keep this in mind: They live in *water*. If you'll turn around and cast your line *this* way—into the water— you'll have a better chance of catching one.

FISHERMAN casts again.

**FISHERMAN**
Don't want one. I'm fishing for men.

ANDREW double takes and then looks to FISHERMAN.

**ANDREW**
If you don't mind me askin', why are you fishing for men?

**Skit Four:**
*Apostle Andrew*

33

FISHERMAN looks at his line.

**FISHERMAN**
A guy at church told me Jesus wants all his followers to do it.

**ANDREW**
I'm glad you feel that way, but I think you're a bit confused, young feller. You see, I'm the Apostle Andrew, and Jesus said those words to *me*.

FISHERMAN bounces a little in excitement.

**FISHERMAN**
(**Excited**) Really? Am I doing it right? Any advice?

ANDREW raises hands and then lowers them to calm down FISHERMAN.

**ANDREW**
Calm down, calm down. I'll tell you all about it. It was back when fishing was my job. I'd heard about Jesus, and one day he walked right over to my boat and told me I should quit fishing for fish and fish for something else.

**FISHERMAN**
He told you to fish for men?

FISHERMAN'S eyes are fixed on ANDREW.

ANDREW looks at FISHERMAN.

**ANDREW**
Yup. Jesus wanted me to fish for men by telling them how much God loves them and *showing* people how much God loves them.

**FISHERMAN**
How'd you get started?

ANDREW faces the audience.

**ANDREW**
I let people see how Jesus had changed me. When my friends asked why I was leaving my boat behind, I said, "I just met Jesus!" I wanted to be with him and do what he wanted.

FISHERMAN continues to look at ANDREW.

**FISHERMAN**
When you fish for men, what do you use for bait?

**ANDREW**
Son, what attracts people to Jesus is love. The Bible says in the book of John, "For God so loved the world that he gave his one and only Son, that whoever believes in him shall not perish but have eternal life. For God did not send his Son into the world to condemn the world, but to save the world through him." That's pretty powerful bait, if you ask me.

FISHERMAN stares in amazement.

**FISHERMAN**
So I just go *tell* people about Jesus? And show them Jesus loves them?

ANDREW looks at FISHERMAN.

**ANDREW**
That's pretty much it.

**FISHERMAN**
I don't need a fishing pole, or bait, or anything?

ANDREW holds his hands out toward FISHERMAN.

**ANDREW**
I think it'll be safer for everyone if you just put the pole down.

FISHERMAN looks around.

**FISHERMAN**
What do I do with the tuna fish sandwiches?

**ANDREW**
How about we have them for lunch and we talk about fishing?

FISHERMAN drops pole. FISHERMAN and ANDREW walk toward STAGE RIGHT.

**FISHERMAN**
So when you were fishing for a living, did you ever snag a big one that got away?

FISHERMAN and ANDREW exit STAGE
RIGHT as ANDREW speaks following line.

**ANDREW**
Son, that's a question you *never* ask a fisherman, not even an apostle...

## For Deeper Learning

Say: **Jesus wants everyone who knows him to tell friends about him.**

Have children form groups of three or four to discuss:

- **Why do you think it's important to tell others about Jesus?**

- **Who told you about Jesus?**

- **What would you tell a friend who asked you to share about Jesus?**

**Skit Four:**
*Apostle Andrew*

# Planning the Wedding

**Bible Reference:** John 2:1-11

## Cast

    **CATERER:** male adult who is assured, pleasant, and smooth, but prone to panic

    **ASSISTANT CATERER:** male adult who is a nice guy but not terribly bright

## Costuming: Caterer wears a Bible-times costume and bow tie. The Assistant Caterer is in a Bible-times costume.

## Props: Bible-times costumes, bow tie

## Setup: Before children arrive for this performance, make one copy of the Wedding Invitation (p. 43) for each child. Distribute the invitations before the play begins.

---

### SCRIPT

| ACTIONS | WORDS |
|---|---|
|  *Play track 5 on CD A.*<br><br>CATERER comes onto stage from STAGE LEFT, moves to CENTER STAGE, and addresses the audience. | **CATERER**<br>Welcome to the wedding feast! Do you have invitations? If you do, please hold them up so I can see them. Hold them up over your heads. Now wave them. OK, that's good. Thank you. Put them down now, and I'll tell you what you've missed.<br><br>As you can hear, the happy couple and their guests are having a great time in the house over there. They're enjoying a truly *spectacular* meal. I know because I'm the caterer. It's my job to make sure there's plenty to eat and drink, and, boy, have *I* been busy! Seems like everyone in *Cana* showed up today. But the more, the merrier, I always say. |
| ASSISTANT leans into sight, STAGE LEFT. | **ASSISTANT**<br>(Stage whisper, urgent) Pssst! Boss! |

| | **CATERER**<br>Excuse me. One of my staff seems to need me. |
| --- | --- |
| CATERER turns to STAGE LEFT. | What's up? |
| | **ASSISTANT**<br>We're running out of wine, boss. |
| CATERER shrugs. | **CATERER**<br>No problem. Open the extra jars we brought into the house. |
| ASSISTANT disappears STAGE LEFT. | **ASSISTANT**<br>OK. Sorry to bother you. |
| CATERER looks back to AUDIENCE. | **CATERER**<br>(To kids) As I was saying, it's *my* job... |
| ASSISTANT reappears STAGE LEFT. | **ASSISTANT**<br>(Stage whisper) Boss! |
| CATERER looks STAGE LEFT. | **CATERER**<br>(Slightly irritated) What now? |
| | **ASSISTANT**<br>I just remembered that I already *did* that. The extra jars are empty too! |
| CATERER flicks his head toward the imaginary wagon. | **CATERER**<br>Then go out to the cart and bring in *those* jars, the backup supply we brought. |
| ASSISTANT disappears STAGE LEFT. | **ASSISTANT**<br>OK, I'm on it! |
| CATERER looks back at audience. | **CATERER**<br>(To audience) It's so hard to get good help these days... |

| | |
|---|---|
| ASSISTANT reappears STAGE LEFT. | **ASSISTANT**<br>(Stage whisper) Boss! Hey, boss! |
| CATERER rounds quickly on ASSISTANT. | **CATERER**<br>(Irritated) *Now* what do you need? |
| | **ASSISTANT**<br>I forgot: I already did *that*, too! Our backup has been used up! |
| CATERER calms down and starts to sound more worried. | **CATERER**<br>So how much wine do we actually have left? |
| ASSISTANT looks up as if to tally in his head. | **ASSISTANT**<br>Well, if you include the jars we brought into the house first, plus our backup supply, and the jar I left in the cart by accident—I guess that would be our *backup* backup supply—and you subtract what people have drunk...um, that leaves us with...let's see...nothing. Not a drop. We're bone dry in there, boss. |
| CATERER drops his head and shakes it in dismay. Then he rushes back and forth on CENTER STAGE. | **CATERER**<br>(Despair) We can't run out of wine at a wedding feast! What will people *say*? What will people *do*? |
| | **VOICE**<br>(Roaring, offstage) Where's that caterer? I'm gonna *throttle* him! |
| ASSISTANT points OFFSTAGE LEFT. | **ASSISTANT**<br>That's the bride's father, and that's pretty much what he's gonna do. |
| | **CATERER**<br>(Urgent) Well, go in and stall them. I'll think of something. |

ASSISTANT disappears STAGE LEFT.

**ASSISTANT**
OK, but think fast.

**CATERER**
(Despair) This is *awful*. These wedding parties can go on for *days*, and having lots to eat and drink is part of the celebration. When you run out of wine, it *really* embarrasses the person putting on the party. We are so sunk. I'll never get hired again if we don't do *something*. But what can we do? I only brought so much wine!

(Baffled) I wonder what *that's* about...

Crowd applauds and cheers through STAGE LEFT channel.

ASSISTANT enters from STAGE LEFT.

**ASSISTANT**
(Excited) Boss! Problem solved!

CATERER looks STAGE LEFT.

**CATERER**
(Baffled) What did you do? Were those people *cheering* you?

**ASSISTANT**
ASSISTANT shakes his head "no."

(Excited) Not me—*Jesus*! He just did the most *amazing* thing. You should've *seen* it!

**CATERER**
Is Jesus one of the guests?

**ASSISTANT**
ASSISTANT nods his head "yes."

Yeah, he came with his mom and some friends.

**CATERER**
CATERER tilts his head.

(Confused) And he brought wine?

**ASSISTANT**
(Excited) No, he *made* wine. Out of *water*! He had some guys fill six stone jars with water. Then, when they dipped out the water, it was *wine*!

CATERER shakes his head slowly.

**CATERER**
(**Astounded**) But that's not possible!

**ASSISTANT**
Maybe not, but it happened! Hear how happy those people are? That's because they saw something amazing—a miracle! And they're drinking the best wine they've ever tasted!

**CATERER**
(**Disbelieving**) You're telling me Jesus made wine out of water?

ASSISTANT nods eagerly.

**ASSISTANT**
Yup!

**CATERER**
(**Doubtful**) And it's *good* wine?

ASSISTANT nods eagerly.

**ASSISTANT**
The banquet master said it's even better than the wine we brought!

**CATERER**
You think Jesus could do this anytime he wanted? Turn water into wine?

**ASSISTANT**
I don't know...maybe. Why?

CATERER looks at audience.

**CATERER**
(**Excited**) Think about it: Water is free and good wine costs lots of money! If Jesus makes me wine for free, and I sell it, I'll get rich! I have to go offer him a job right now! He's inside?

**ASSISTANT**
Yeah, he was by the buffet table the last time I looked.

CATERER continues to look at audience.

**CATERER**
Thanks again for coming. My assistant here can take care of getting you some food. I have to go interview someone I want to hire!

CATERER rushes off STAGE LEFT.

**ASSISTANT**
Um, OK boss.

Uh, does anyone here like chocolate cake? Great! I'd get you some, but we ran out of that, too.

ASSISTANT moves to CENTER STAGE from STAGE LEFT. He delivers his first line as he looks over his shoulder.
ASSISTANT looks at audience.
ASSISTANT laughs a large silent laugh.

**(Idea dawning)** Hey, maybe Jesus does *cake*! I'll go check; you wait here!

**ASSISTANT**
Nope. Sorry. Guess you're out of luck. Jesus doesn't do miracles to make money. They said he does miracles to help people and to help them believe. Well, I gotta go back to work. 'Bye!

ASSISTANT rushes off STAGE LEFT.
ASSISTANT after 5 second pause sticks head onto stage from STAGE LEFT.

ASSISTANT exits STAGE LEFT.

## For Deeper Learning

Say: **Our friend, the Caterer, thinks he can convince Jesus to do miracles for money, but that's not why Jesus did miracles. He did them to show the power of God.**

**Jesus could do things that nobody else could do—that's what working miracles means.**

Have children form groups of three or four to discuss:

- **How would you have felt if you'd been at this wedding and seen Jesus turn water into wine?**

- **How does knowing that Jesus can do amazing things make you feel? Why?**

- **What's an amazing thing that God has done in your life or the life of someone you know?**

**Skit Five:**
*Planning the Wedding*

# You are invited...

*Please join us in Cana as we celebrate the marriage of Anna and Joseph.*

*Lots to eat, lots to drink, and lots of fun!*

*Bring this invitation with you to confirm that you're a guest, please.*

# You are invited...

*Please join us in Cana as we celebrate the marriage of Anna and Joseph.*

*Lots to eat, lots to drink, and lots of fun!*

*Bring this invitation with you to confirm that you're a guest, please.*

# Friend of the Paralytic

**Bible Reference:** Mark 2:1-12

**Cast**

    ELIAS: elderly, grumpy Jewish man

    FRIEND: young man

**Costuming:** Both Elias and Friend wear Bible-times costumes.

**Props:** Bible-times costumes, walking cane (appropriate length of dowel) carried by Elias

---

## SCRIPT

| ACTIONS | WORDS |
|---|---|
| 💿 *Play track 6 on CD A.* | |
| ELIAS enters STAGE RIGHT and moves to CENTER STAGE as he speaks. | **ELIAS**<br>**(Grumpy old man grousing to audience)** The crowds here in Capernaum are getting worse and worse. Too many people, that's what I say. Too many *teenagers*! *Vandals*, all of them—writing on the walls, ripping up decent people's houses... |
| | **FRIEND**<br>**(Offstage. Out of breath)** Gotta hurry... |
| FRIEND dashes in from STAGE LEFT and runs into ELIAS. Both puppets fall flat. | **ELIAS**<br>This neighborhood just isn't the same anymore. Why, back in the old days, it used to... |
| FRIEND looks up. | **FRIEND**<br>Huh? |
| FRIEND looks at ELIAS. | **ELIAS**<br>**(Groaning)** Oooofff! |

Both puppets lie flat for two seconds, then ELIAS gets up, slowly shakes his head, and looks at FRIEND, who also slowly gets up.

FRIEND gets up from collision.

ELIAS dusts himself off.

ELIAS points to STAGE RIGHT.

FRIEND looks left and right and then back to ELIAS.

**FRIEND**
(**Groaning**) Ohhhhhhhhhhh.

**ELIAS**
(**Indignant**) Hey, watch where you're going! You almost *killed* me!

**FRIEND**
(**In pain but OK**) Sorry...I was in a hurry. I'm supposed to meet some friends...

**ELIAS**
(**Still miffed**) Well, you'll be meeting them in the *hospital* if you don't slow down! And you'll send *me* there, too!

**FRIEND**
(**Still in pain, but also in a hurry**) I *said* I was sorry...I know you probably can't help me, but I'm looking for the house where Jesus is staying.

**ELIAS**
Well, it's over there—the house with the crowd around it. The crowd making all that hullabaloo.

**FRIEND**
Thanks! Did you happen to see four guys pass by here carrying a man who's crippled? The crippled guy is skinny and has curly hair and a beard, and he'd be wearing a blue robe. They'd be going to that house.

**ELIAS**
(**Suspicious**) Are you with them?

**FRIEND**
They're friends of mine. I was supposed to help carry our buddy over there, but I was late.

| | |
|---|---|
| ELIAS takes an angry step toward FRIEND, who backs up a step. | **ELIAS**<br>(Indignant) So *that's* it! You're one of the *vandals*! You should be *ashamed*! |
| | **FRIEND**<br>(Puzzled) I don't understand... |
| FRIEND looks left and right for an escape. | |
| ELIAS shakes his cane. | **ELIAS**<br>(Excited and angry) Your hoodlum *friends* couldn't get in to see Jesus. So they carried that curly-haired guy up on the roof, and they tore a *hole* in the roof! |
| FRIEND keeps his eyes on ELIAS. | **FRIEND**<br>Really? |
| | **ELIAS**<br>What? Like I'd make this *up*? Yes, really! A perfectly fine roof—ruined! Your friends lowered your crippled buddy down through the hole. |
| | **FRIEND**<br>What did Jesus do? |
| ELIAS drops his cane. | **ELIAS**<br>(Grudgingly) I guess Jesus appreciates it when people show they really believe in him. So he forgave your friend's sins. And then he healed him. |
| FRIEND leans closer. | **FRIEND**<br>Healed him? Healed him! How? |
| | **ELIAS**<br>(Impatiently) Healed him like ten minutes ago he went jumping and dancing down the street with your hoodlum friends hooting and hollering along with him. Disturbing the peace, all of them! I should've called the police! |

FRIEND jumps with joy.

**FRIEND**
(Delighted) That's *great*! We *knew* Jesus could do it! When you're with Jesus, you can just feel his power. He really *is* the Son of God! Which way did my friends go?

ELIAS points STAGE RIGHT.

**ELIAS**
That way. And moving too fast, if you ask me.

FRIEND rushes off STAGE RIGHT.

**FRIEND**
Thanks! I've got to catch them!

ELIAS calls STAGE RIGHT.

**ELIAS**
(Calling) Slow down! You're a menace! And tell your friends they have a roof to repair!

(Muttering) Aye, aye, aye. Kids these days. Why, back when I was a boy, people were *polite*. None of this running down the street like their sandals are on fire...

ELIAS exits STAGE LEFT.

## For Deeper Learning

Say: **I think our elderly friend is having a bad day. Let's hope he meets Jesus and cheers up!**

You know, when people were with Jesus, interesting things happened. In this situation, Jesus forgave the sins of a paralyzed man. When religious leaders said that nobody but God could forgive sins, Jesus asked what would be easier—to forgive sins or heal the man's body. Then Jesus healed the man's body.

Jesus is powerful! He can forgive sins and make crippled people walk!

Have children form groups of three or four and discuss:

- **If you'd been the crippled man Jesus healed, how would you have felt?**
- **Why do you think Jesus decided to help the crippled man?**
- **What's something powerful Jesus has done in your life?**

# Clear the Temple

**Bible Reference:** John 2:13-17

## Cast

> **TOURIST:** wide-eyed, innocent male in the big city
> **CONSTRUCTION WORKER:** gruff and distracted adult male
> **JOE:** direct but thoughtful adult male

## Costuming:
The Tourist is dressed in a Bible-times costume, with a disposable camera tied around his neck. The Construction Worker wears a Bible-times costume and a hard hat and carries a board. Joe wears a Bible-times costume.

## Props:
Bible-times costumes, small disposable camera, hard hat, board

---

**SCRIPT**

| ACTIONS | WORDS |
|---|---|
|  *Play track 7 on CD A.*<br><br>TOURIST enters from STAGE LEFT and goes to CENTER STAGE.<br><br><br>From OFFSTAGE: a loud moo, a thud, and a dog yelping.<br><br>TOURIST looks at the noise, then turns back to the audience. | **TOURIST**<br>Ladies and gentlemen, the show's producer, director, and cast want me to make a brief announcement. Although animals are featured in our show today, none were injured at any time...<br><br>Except for that dog, and since he was chasing cattle, he pretty much got what he deserved.<br><br>This play also called for us to build an exact replica of the Temple in Jerusalem as it appeared in Jesus' day. That was going to cost about four hundred twelve million dollars, so instead we're asking you to use your imaginations. Let me give you a tour. |
| TOURIST moves to STAGE RIGHT and points OFFSTAGE RIGHT. | Over there is the Temple. It's made of white marble and gold, and it's *huge*. It took nearly twenty years to build it. |

TOURIST moves to CENTER STAGE.

ANIMALS make sounds of concern from OFFSTAGE.

TOURIST calls OFFSTAGE RIGHT.

Out here is the market where people visiting the Temple can trade their Roman money in for money to pay the Temple tax. And here's where you can buy animals to sacrifice.

Not any of you—it's OK!

**(Aside)** Actors are so *touchy*.

**(Resuming tour voice)** The city of Jerusalem is all around us because we're up on a hill. Look around and see all the people with you. They're people who live in Jerusalem.

I'm going to go get ready for my big entrance. Thanks for taking the tour and for saving us millions of dollars.

TOURIST goes off STAGE LEFT.

**(Loud whisper from offstage)** Shhhh! Everyone quiet down!

Sheep bleats from OFFSTAGE.

**(Loud whisper from offstage)** You too!

TOURIST enters STAGE LEFT, glances up and around.

# TOURIST
Boy, I've always wanted to see the Temple, and now here I am. The glory! The grandeur! The *mess*! It looks like there was a *riot* here...

WORKER enters from STAGE RIGHT carrying board.

# WORKER
Watch out! Busy construction worker comin' through!

TOURIST looks around and then looks at WORKER.

# TOURIST
Excuse me, but what happened? Earthquake? Tornado? Slumber party? It looks *awful*!

WORKER looks around almost smacking TOURIST in the head with the board.

# WORKER
Don't blame me; we're cleanin' up as fast as we can!

| | |
|---|---|
| TOURIST continues to look around. | **TOURIST**<br>Is this the marketplace? |
| WORKER pauses and looks at TOURIST. | **WORKER**<br>It was until about four hours ago. That's when some guy started turning over tables and throwing money around and letting animals go free. |
| TOURIST and WORKER look OFFSTAGE RIGHT to watch what JOE is up to, then turn back to face each other. | **JOE**<br>(Yelling from offstage) Hey! Get that sheep *outta* here! |
| | **TOURIST**<br>Who did it? |
| WORKER looks OFFSTAGE RIGHT and calls. | **WORKER**<br>I dunno. Wasn't here. Maybe Joe can tell you. (Calling) Hey, Joe! |
| | **JOE**<br>(From offstage) What? |
| WORKER'S mouth wide as he yells. | **WORKER**<br>(Yelling stage right) Some guy wants to talk with you! |
| | **JOE**<br>(From offstage) Be right there! |
| WORKER continues toward STAGE LEFT and exits. | **WORKER**<br>See you later, Bub. |
| TOURIST calls to WORKER. | **TOURIST**<br>Thanks! |
| Turns to audience. | (To self) Boy, it didn't look like *this* in the travel brochures... |

JOE enters STAGE RIGHT. Yells to OFFSTAGE RIGHT.

**JOE**
Take care of those busted up birdcages! And do something with the cattle!

**VOICE 1**
(From offstage) Sure thing, boss!

JOE turns from talking to voice off stage and looks at TOURIST.

**JOE**
(Businesslike) What can I do for you? You from the Temple Office?

**TOURIST**
No, I was wondering...

JOE shakes his head "no" then motions OFFSTAGE to point to all the damage.

**JOE**
Oh, I get it—you're a *tourist*. Well, here's what you missed: A few hours ago, a guy named Jesus came through this marketplace and tore the whole place up. And now me and my guys are trying to put it back together. End of story.

**VOICE 2**
(From offstage) Hey! Those doves did that on *purpose*!

JOE and TOURIST both shake their heads in disgust.

**TOURIST**
Why did Jesus wreck the market?

TOURIST looks at JOE.

JOE gestures and moves around stage as he explains.

**JOE**
He said the Temple should be a house of prayer and we'd turned it into a market. Which was *true*, when you think about it. He made a whip out of some rope and started a cattle stampede. Turned tables over so there was money everywhere. It was pretty exciting.

**TOURIST**
Aren't you mad at Jesus for making such a mess?

| | |
|---|---|
| JOE looks up as if thinking. | **JOE**<br>**(Thoughtful)** At first I was, but then I got to thinking. The Temple *is* supposed to be a house of prayer, just like Jesus said. Out here it was more like a circus. |
| | **TOURIST**<br>Still, when someone tips over tables, shouldn't you lock him up? |
| JOE points to TOURIST. | **JOE**<br>Let me ask you a question: If you came to my house to visit me, who would you expect to see? |
| TOURIST scratches his head. | **TOURIST**<br>Um...you, I guess. |
| JOE moves closer to TOURIST. | **JOE**<br>Who would you expect to *talk* to? |
| | **TOURIST**<br>You. |
| JOE moves even closer to TOURIST. | **JOE**<br>Who would you expect to spend *time* with? |
| | **TOURIST**<br>Well, if I came to *your* house, to see you, I'd expect to spend time with *you*. |
| JOE pokes TOURIST in the chest to make his point. | **JOE**<br>So maybe when you come to visit the Temple, God's house, you should expect to talk to *God*. Spend time with *God*. Not buy and sell stuff, especially stuff that's overpriced like all this was. People got cheated all the time. |

Hey, I was here. I just met Jesus, and I'll tell you, he made a lot of sense. Not that I want him doing this kind of thing every *day*. But maybe if people listen to him, he won't have to. Gotta get back to work, Mac. Have a good day.

**(From offstage)** Don't *milk* 'em; *move* 'em!

## TOURIST

House of prayer, huh? Good idea. I think I'll go pray before I take more pictures.

## VOICE 1

**(Calling from offstage)** I said get back in the pen. Hey! Back in the pen!

## TOURIST

And before I get run over by a herd of sheep!

JOE exits STAGE RIGHT.

TOURIST steps back as if he were about to be run over from STAGE LEFT to STAGE RIGHT.

TOURIST hurries off STAGE RIGHT.

## For Deeper Learning

Say: **Because of the Temple rules, there needed to be a place for visitors to exchange their money for special Temple money. And visitors needed a place to buy animals for sacrifices.**

**But Jesus didn't want the merchants to cheat people or to distract them from worshipping God!**

**When we go to church, it's easy for us to get busy doing something else when it's time for worshipping God. Sometimes we turn our time with God into something else, too.**

Have children form groups of three or four to discuss:

- **How do you think the merchants felt when Jesus turned over tables and set animals free?**
- **Why do you think Jesus was angry about the merchants?**
- **What things distract you from thinking about God when you're at church? Why?**

# Nicodemus

**Bible Reference:** John 3:1-21

## Cast

**MAN:** somewhat excitable adult male

**NICODEMUS:** adult male who takes himself seriously, trying to not be spotted

## Costuming: 
Man and Nicodemus wear Bible-times costumes. Nicodemus wears a headdress or turban, trying to hide his identity.

## Props: 
Bible-times costumes

## Setup: 
Just before the play begins, slowly dim the lights so that the stage is in semi-darkness. Allow time for kids' eyes to adjust, and be sure there's enough light so the audience can see the action.

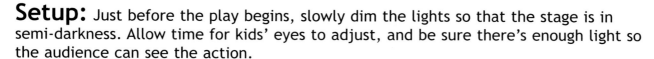

| ACTIONS | WORDS |
|---------|-------|
| 💿 *Play track 8 on CD A.* | |
| MAN strolls slowly on stage from STAGE LEFT, humming to self. He pauses. | **MAN**<br>Dum, de dum, de dum de dum...<br><br>**(Takes a deep breath and exhales with a satisfied sigh)** Ah, Jerusalem at midnight. Great time for a walk. The streets are so *crowded* during the day... |
| MAN sighs and resumes moving. | **(Sighs)** |
| | **TOWN CRIER**<br>**(Calling from offstage)** 11:45 and all is well! |
| NICODEMUS enters from STAGE RIGHT. NICODEMUS and MAN speak before they pass each other. | **MAN**<br>**(Agreeably)** Hi. Nice night for a stroll. |
| NICODEMUS drops his head a little so as not to be recognized. | **NICODEMUS**<br>Yes. Very nice, very nice. |

| | |
|---|---|
| MAN takes a few more steps and then turns and calls to NICODEMUS. | **MAN**<br>(Thoughtful) Wait a minute. Do I know you? |
| | **NICODEMUS**<br>(Hurriedly) No, I'm sure you don't. Good night. |
| NICODEMUS doesn't turn to face MAN. | |
| MAN approaches NICODEMUS, who is still trying to not be recognized. | **MAN**<br>(Thoughtfully) I never forget a face. I'm sure I've seen you somewhere...<br><br>(Pause)<br><br>(Excitedly) Hey, you're Nicodemus the Pharisee, right? You're in Jerusalem's council of rulers! I see you all the time up at the Temple! |
| NICODEMUS looks around to see who's watching. | **NICODEMUS**<br>Well, I may *look* like him... |
| | **MAN**<br>C'mon, you're Nicodemus! I'd know you anywhere. Why the disguise?<br><br>(Voice drops to conspiratorial stage whisper.) You on some kind of top-secret council of rulers *spy* mission? |
| NICODEMUS shakes his head "no." | **NICODEMUS**<br>No, no spy mission... |
| | **MAN**<br>You running away from home? |
| NICODEMUS stops shaking his head and looks at MAN. | **NICODEMUS**<br>(Indignant) Of course not! |
| | **MAN**<br>Oh, *I* get it: You don't want people asking you for autographs! Well, I think you're |

safe; nobody around except you and me. Um, say, it doesn't seem like there'd be a lot of *demand* for Pharisee autographs. You get asked a lot?

## NICODEMUS
I'm *not* hiding from autograph hunters! The fact is...

MAN and NICODEMUS turn to look STAGE RIGHT when TOWN CRIER speaks.

## TOWN CRIER
(Calling from offstage) Weather update: It's not raining!

MAN turns back to NICODEMUS.

## MAN
You were saying?

NICODEMUS drops head.

## NICODEMUS
(Defensively) I was *saying*...(sigh)

NICODEMUS looks MAN in the eye.

(Decides to come clean) I was saying that I'm wearing a disguise because I don't want my Pharisee friends to see me here.

## MAN
Why? You owe them money?

NICODEMUS shakes his head "no."

## NICODEMUS
No.

MAN looks around to see if anyone is watching.

## MAN
You borrow their camel and take it back all out of gas?

## NICODEMUS
(Growing impatient) No!

MAN steps toward NICODEMUS.

## MAN
You did *something* wrong, didn't you?

## NICODEMUS
(Defensively) No! I mean...yes! No! Well...sort of. Maybe.

**MAN**

I didn't think you Pharisees *ever* did anything wrong. I thought you *always* obeyed the rules.

**NICODEMUS**

We do. At least, we *try* to.

**MAN**

So what did you do? You can tell me.

**NICODEMUS**

(**Being vulnerable**) It wasn't wrong, but I think, if they think, they might *think* it was wrong. Do you know what I mean?

**MAN**

Not really, but keep going. Maybe I can catch up.

**NICODEMUS**

(**Marveling**) Tonight I met the most amazing man. A teacher. His name is Jesus.

**MAN**

So...what does he teach?

**TOWN CRIER**

(**Calling from offstage**) Chariot race scores just in: Galilee Galleons 21, Roman Stallions X, X, V!

**NICODEMUS**

(**Marveling**) That's just it: We know he's a teacher who comes from God and who teaches about God. But some people say he's the *Son* of God. I just had to find out, even if my Pharisee friends thought I was crazy.

Now NICODEMUS looks around to see if anyone is watching.

MAN comes closer to hear the secret.

MAN looks at audience.

MAN and NICODEMUS turn to look STAGE RIGHT when TOWN CRIER speaks.

**Skit Eight:**
Nicodemus

**MAN**
So what did you decide? *Is* Jesus the Son of God?

NICODEMUS nods his head "yes."

**NICODEMUS**
I...I think he might *be* the Son of God! He can do things nobody else can do! He knows things that nobody else could know! And he loves us—all of us.

**MAN**
Are you going to tell your friends who he is?

**NICODEMUS**
Maybe...but not tonight. Look, I've said too much already. You can't tell anyone that you saw me. Not a word, you understand?

MAN looks around to see if anyone is listening.

**MAN**
Me? Not a word. I understand.

NICODEMUS looks straight at MAN.

**NICODEMUS**
You didn't see me tonight, you didn't *talk* with me, you don't know where I've been.

**MAN**
Didn't see you, didn't talk with you, don't know a thing about Jesus. Got it. Trust me, I can keep my mouth shut. They can ask me questions, and I won't say *anything*. Not a word. They can offer me *money*, and I won't tell them what I know. They can make me stand in the street and run *chariot* wheels over my toes, and I won't make a peep. They can...

**NICODEMUS**
Fine, fine...just run along. Finish your stroll. I need some time to myself.

MAN resumes walk, talking to self until OFFSTAGE.

NICODEMUS looks up.

**MAN**
You got it!

Not a word to *anybody*. Not a *peep*. Not one word. No way, no how...no siree...

**NICODEMUS**
I think I met God's Son tonight. I think I met my Savior. I just met Jesus. What I need to know is should I tell the others? What if they find out that I went to see Jesus? If they find out I *believe* in Jesus?

**TOWN CRIER**
**(Calling from offstage)** News flash: Top Pharisee Nicodemus meets with Jesus! Details in the morning!

NICODEMUS is still looking up.

NICODEMUS resumes direction and walks OFFSTAGE.

**NICODEMUS**
Well, I guess I have my answer...

## For Deeper Learning

Say: **Nicodemus was excited about meeting Jesus, but he knew following Jesus would mean he had to make some hard choices. When we follow Jesus, it means we have to make some choices too.**

Have children form groups of three or four to discuss:

- **Why do you think Nicodemus wanted to stay hidden?**
- **How do you think Nicodemus felt the night he met Jesus? Why?**
- **What choices do you think you'll have to make to follow Jesus?**

# Centurion and Servant

**Bible Reference:** Matthew 8:5-13

## Cast

**CENTURION:** adult male Roman who has an authoritative air

**SERVANT:** adult male who is excited to be carrying good news

**NARRATOR:** offstage speaker who sets the stage

**Costuming:** The Roman Centurion wears a white Bible-times costume with a red tunic over it. The Servant wears a Bible-times costume.

**Props:** Bible-times costumes, tunic, sword (You can create this by putting plastic or aluminum foil over cardboard.)

**Setup:** Before the play begins, drop the lighting in the room until the Narrator finishes speaking.

---

### SCRIPT

| ACTIONS | WORDS |
|---|---|
| 💿 *Play track 9 on CD A.* | **NARRATOR**<br>When Jesus had entered Capernaum, a centurion—a soldier who commanded one hundred men—came to him asking for help. "Lord," he said, "my servant lies at home paralyzed and in terrible suffering." Jesus said to him, "I'll go and heal him."<br><br>But the centurion replied, "Lord, I don't deserve to have you come under my roof. But just say the word and my servant will be healed. I understand authority because I have soldiers under me. I tell them what to do and they do it. I know you have authority too."<br><br>When Jesus heard this, he said to those following him, "I tell you the truth: I haven't found anyone in Israel with such great faith." Jesus said to the centurion, |
| ROMAN CENTURION enters STAGE LEFT and moves toward CENTER STAGE. | |

SERVANT runs on STAGE RIGHT and meets ROMAN CENTURION at CENTER STAGE.

SERVANT enters huffing and puffing from STAGE RIGHT and crosses to face CENTURION.

CENTURION reaches out to comfort SERVANT.

CENTURION drops his hand.

CENTURION confidently nods his head "yes."

SERVANT double takes CENTURION and audience.

SERVANT raises his hands in amazement.

"Go! It will be done just as you believed it would."

**SERVANT**
**(Panting, fighting for breath)** Boss! Boss! I have...I have...

**ROMAN CENTURION**
Catch your breath, Darion! Did you run all the way from home?

**SERVANT**
**(Getting breathing under control)** Yeah...all the way...from home...whew!

**ROMAN CENTURION**
And you have news about Marcus, my sick servant.

**SERVANT**
**(Breathing becoming normal now)** See, I have news about Marcus. See, he's...Hey, how could you know that?

**ROMAN CENTURION**
And it's good news.

**SERVANT**
**(Impatiently)** You ain't gonna believe it, but it's...um, it's good news. How...?

**ROMAN CENTURION**
He was suddenly healed. Completely back to normal. In fact, he's *better* than normal, right?

**SERVANT**
**(Amazed)** Yeah, but how could you possibly *know* that? When you left, the doctors all said Marcus was gonna *die*. He couldn't even sit *up*!

CENTURION turns to audience and drops his head.

SERVANT double takes audience and CENTURION.

**ROMAN CENTURION**
Well, he's better now, thank God.

**SERVANT**
(**Amazed**) Don't get me wrong; we're all really *glad* about that. Me, your wife, the other servants, everyone. *Especially* Marcus! But how could *you* know that he was healed when you weren't there? You go off to see that guy...

**ROMAN CENTURION**
Jesus.

SERVANT nods his head "yes."

**SERVANT**
Yeah, him. You go see Jesus and then while you're gone, one minute Marcus is lying there like any second he's gonna die, and then the next minute he's up wondering what we're all staring at. Nobody's ever seen anything like it!

CENTURION looks at SERVANT.

**ROMAN CENTURION**
The reason I know it happened is that Jesus *told* me it would happen. Just like I believed it would.

**SERVANT**
This Jesus healed Marcus? From all the way over in the next town? No way!

**ROMAN CENTURION**
Jesus has the power to do it, like I have the power to order my soldiers to march or to set up camp.

SERVANT shakes his head "no."

**SERVANT**
(**Disbelieving**) Yeah, boss, but *heal* someone? Come on...

CENTURION nods his head "yes."

SERVANT raises and lowers his hands in disbelief.

SERVANT raises his hands to CENTURION.

CENTURION points OFFSTAGE.

SERVANT shakes his head "no."

CENTURION seems to get a little taller.

SERVANT nods his head "yes."

DARION turns and starts running. Exits STAGE RIGHT.

## ROMAN CENTURION

It's true. I just met Jesus, and I saw him order Marcus to get better. You saw it happen with your own eyes.

## SERVANT

(Disbelieving) Still, you can't just *order* someone to get better...

## ROMAN CENTURION

Tell you what, Darion: Let me give you a little demonstration. Jesus is so powerful that he can order people to get better. I can't do that, but I can order you to run all the way back home.

## SERVANT

(Protesting) But, boss! Do you know how *far* that is? And I just ran *here*!

## ROMAN CENTURION

Start moving. Tell them I'll be home soon.

## SERVANT

(Whining) But, *boss*...

## ROMAN CENTURION

(Sternly) *Now*, Darion.

## SERVANT

(Resigned) Yes, sir...I'm on my way...

## ROMAN CENTURION

(To audience) Maybe you think I was too hard on old Darion? Making him run all those miles? Well, he needs to understand that I have the power to make him obey orders...just like Jesus has the power over Marcus' illness. Jesus is more powerful than *anything*.

CENTURION exits STAGE RIGHT.

Well, I'm heading home to see Marcus. God bless you!

## For Deeper Learning

Say: **Jesus is powerful! But Jesus showed us that something else is powerful, too: the faith of the Centurion. Jesus was amazed at how much the man believed in him! The Centurion didn't have any doubt that Jesus could just say the word and a servant many miles away would be healed.**

Have children form groups of three or four and discuss:

- How strong is your faith? Is it tiny, middle-sized, or huge? Why do you describe it the way you do?

- What's something in the world that you believe in—no questions asked? Why do you believe in it?

- What's something you're trusting Jesus to do?

# Fish and Loaves

**Bible Reference:** John 6:1-15

## Cast

**HOT DOG SALESMAN:** adult male who is baffled by what's happening

**BOY:** innocent and happy young male

## Costuming: Hot Dog Salesman wears a Bible-times costume and a baseball cap. On the front of the baseball cap is a white card on which is written in block letters: "HOT DOGS." Dress Boy in a Bible-times costume.

## Props: Bible-times costumes, baseball cap, small sign that says "HOT DOGS"

---

### SCRIPT

| ACTIONS | WORDS |
|---|---|
|  **Play track 10 on CD A.** | |
| HOT DOG SALESMAN enters from STAGE LEFT and crosses to CENTER STAGE to address audience. | **HOT DOG SALESMAN**<br>**(To audience)** I'm glad you're all here for our show! We had a few thousand actors phone in sick, so you're going to have to take their roles. Don't worry, it's nothing hard. You just have to look like you've eaten so much that you can hardly move. Here's what you do. First, everyone puff out your cheeks. Now roll your eyes around like you're about to fall over. Now put your hands on your foreheads like you're saying, "I can't believe I ate all that!" Then moan a little. **(5 second pause)**<br><br>Great! Perfect! Now just go back to being a regular, wonderful audience. Don't do any of that until you hear me say, "And just look at all of them! They've eaten so much, they can hardly move!" That's your cue! See you in a minute. |
| HOT DOG SALESMAN quickly exits STAGE LEFT. | |

HOT DOG SALESMAN enters from STAGE LEFT and crosses to CENTER STAGE.

HOT DOG SALESMAN puts his hands to his mouth.

(From offstage) OK, roll the sound effects tape!

## HOT DOG SALESMAN
(Shouting) Hot dogs! Get your hot dogs! Get your red-hot hot dogs right here!

## VOICE 1
(Moaning from offstage) Oh, man! I am *so* full.

## VOICE 2
(From offstage) Hot dogs? Who'd want a hot dog after all *this*?

## VOICE 3
(From offstage) I am *stuffed*!

## HOT DOG SALESMAN
(To audience) I don't get it. Thousands of people who've been standing out here in the middle of nowhere *all* day with *no* food, and *I* can't sell hot dogs! What is *up* with this? I thought I'd be busier than a publican at tax time!

SALESMAN looks STAGE RIGHT to watch BOY enter.

## HOT DOG SALESMAN
(Calling) Hey, boy! Hey, you! Boy!

BOY looks at SALESMAN.

## BOY
Me?

SALESMAN nods his head "yes" and raises his hand toward the audience.

## HOT DOG SALESMAN
Yeah. What's going *on* here? Why isn't anybody hungry?

BOY rubs his tummy as if full.

## BOY
Well, they just had lunch.

SALESMAN looks left and right to look for other food vendors.

## HOT DOG SALESMAN
(Baffled) Lunch? Where'd they get *lunch*? What did they find to eat way out here?

BOY looks at SALESMAN.

SALESMAN stops looking around to look at BOY.

BOY looks at SALESMAN.

SALESMAN looks at BOY and gestures toward audience.

BOY looks at audience and then back to SALESMAN.

SALESMAN looks up and down as if sizing up how much the BOY could really eat.

BOY just stands there looking at the SALESMAN.

SALESMAN looks at audience and then back at the BOY.

BOY continues to look at the SALESMAN.

HOT DOG SALESMAN points to the audience.

## BOY
Fish sandwiches.

## HOT DOG SALESMAN
Fish sandwiches? I thought I was the only food salesman out here!

## BOY
You are.

## HOT DOG SALESMAN
Then where did all these people buy sandwiches?

## BOY
They didn't buy them. The bread and fish were free. These people shared the lunch my mom packed for me.

## HOT DOG SALESMAN
What'd your mother *pack* for you? A whale on a seven-ton bun? Ha. Ha. Ha.

## BOY
No, just two little fish and five loaves of barley bread.

## HOT DOG SALESMAN
(Incredulous) You're telling me that five loaves of bread and two fish fed *all* these people? There must be three, four thousand people!

## BOY
(Matter-of-fact) Five thousand men plus women and kids. The guys with Jesus counted them.

## HOT DOG SALESMAN
And just look at all of them! They've eaten so much they can hardly move!

Jesus is the guy everyone came to see, right? The star of the show? So what was he doing with your lunch?

**BOY**

Well, when he finished teaching, he noticed that people were hungry. I was the only one who brought lunch, I guess.

**HOT DOG SALESMAN**

I was *counting* on people forgetting food! That's why I'm standing here with seventy-three cases of hot dogs!

**BOY**

Jesus told his disciples to find something for the crowd to eat. One of the disciples, Andrew, found out I had two little fish and five little loaves of bread. Andrew took me right up to Jesus.

**HOT DOG SALESMAN**

You actually went right up to him?

**BOY**

Yeah, I met Jesus. We talked for a minute or two.

**HOT DOG SALESMAN**

What did Jesus do?

**BOY**

He prayed, and then his disciples told everyone to sit down. Jesus started breaking up the fish and bread into pieces. He just kept breaking and breaking and breaking...Then the disciples passed around the pieces and everyone— the whole crowd—had plenty to eat.

---

BOY looks out at audience and then back to SALESMAN.

SALESMAN looks down and then out to audience.

BOY looks at SALESMAN.

SALESMAN looks at BOY.

BOY slowly nods his head "yes."

SALESMAN looks at BOY.

BOY looks to audience.

**Skit Ten:**
*Fish and Loaves*

SALESMAN looks down at his feet.

BOY raises arms out to side as if to say, "Duh!"

SALESMAN looks around and raises his hands.

BOY shakes his head "no."

HOT DOG SALESMAN moves toward STAGE RIGHT as he speaks and exits STAGE RIGHT.

BOY shrugs and exits STAGE LEFT.

## HOT DOG SALESMAN
(Unbelieving) But how could that *work*? There's no *way* that could work!

## BOY
(Excited) It was a miracle! Everybody ate all they wanted, and there were *still* twelve baskets of food left over!

## HOT DOG SALESMAN
So what am I supposed to do with all these hot dogs? They'll never last until I get back to town. They're all gonna spoil!

## BOY
I don't know, but nobody will want to *eat* them. Maybe people can do something else with them.

## HOT DOG SALESMAN
Like what? It's not like you can use hot dogs for...for...

(An idea dawns) Hey, *I* know! I can sell them as *souvenirs*! Thanks for the idea kid!

Get your official Multiplying Fish Souvenirs here! Official Multiplying Fish Souvenirs here! The only official souvenirs between here and town...

## HOT DOG SALESMAN
(From offstage) Yes, sir! One official souvenir coming right up. You want ketchup and relish with that?

## For Deeper Learning

Say: Thousands of people had traveled to hear Jesus teach, and they were *way* out in the country. There wasn't any place for people to buy food. People were hungry! Their tummies were rumbling!

When Jesus saw that the crowd was hungry, he helped them by making a few fish and five little loaves of bread feed more than five thousand people!

Jesus met their needs, and Jesus meets our needs.

Have children form groups of three or four and discuss:

- What's something Jesus has done for you in your life?
- How does it feel knowing that Jesus loves you and wants to help you?
- What's something you want Jesus to help you with this week?

**Skit Ten:**
Fish and Loaves

# Peter on the Water

**Bible Reference:** Matthew 14:22-33

## Cast

**DISCIPLE 1:** adult male who feels the wonder of what he's witnessing

**DISCIPLE 2:** adult male who is a bit cynical, well aware they're in deep trouble

**PETER:** adult male who is a bit enamoured with the notion of being in command

**NARRATOR:** offstage voice who sets the stage for the skit

## Costuming: All puppets wear Bible-times costumes.

## Props: Fan, spray bottle of water, cardboard boat (A flat piece of cardboard the disciples will stand behind will work well. Consider it another puppet that will have to be rocked back and forth and moved slightly.)

## Setup: Place a small fan STAGE LEFT blowing toward STAGE RIGHT so there will be a breeze on stage.

---

**SCRIPT**

| ACTIONS | WORDS |
|---|---|
|  *Play track 1 on CD B.* | |
| DISCIPLE 1 enters from STAGE RIGHT, leaning into the wind. He crosses to CENTER STAGE and addresses the audience. | **DISCIPLE 1** <br> **(Voice raised to be heard above the storm)** Thanks for coming to our show. We thought we might have to cancel it because of this incredible storm, but then we remembered that our show is *about* a storm! So this is sort of like cheap special effects. Keep your heads down and watch out for sea spray. We'll get started in a minute. |
| DISCIPLE 1 exits STAGE RIGHT. | |
| | **NARRATOR** <br> **(From offstage)** Jesus had his disciples get into a boat and go on ahead of him across the Sea of Galilee. Jesus stayed behind so he could finish talking with the |

A BOAT appears STAGE RIGHT, bobbing up and down. In the BOAT (behind it) are—facing STAGE LEFT and in this order—PETER (who stands tall in the bow of the boat facing STAGE LEFT), DISCIPLE 2 (who's facing STAGE RIGHT and is moving back and forth as if he's rowing) and DISCIPLE 1 (who's in the rear of the boat and is ducking up and down as if he's bailing water).

DISCIPLE 2 moves as if he is rowing a boat.

PETER is bobbing with the boat.

BOAT rocks backward severely as puppeteer sprays water out over audience.

DISCIPLE 2 turns to DISCIPLE 1.

crowds and then go up into the hills for a time of prayer.

The disciples did as Jesus asked, and when evening came the boat was already far from shore, tossed about on the rising swells. The wind beat the waves into froth and pounded the little boat. And it was the middle of the night...

## PETER
**(Speaking with a voice of command)** Pull! Pull! Pull! You're going to have to row harder than *that* if we're going to get to shore by morning...

## DISCIPLE 2
**(Breathlessly)** How come I'm doin' all the rowin'?

## PETER
**(Majestically)** *Somebody* has to keep a lookout to make sure we don't hit anything.

## DISCIPLE 1
What could we possibly hit, Peter? Who *else* is dumb enough to be out here in the middle of a windstorm?

**(Surprised)** Whoooa! *That* was a big wave!

## PETER
**(Majestically, into the wind)** Now, men, be stouthearted! This isn't a time for mutiny. Bend your backs, hoist the mainsail, and let us *fly* before the wind, me mateys!

## DISCIPLE 2
Peter has been reading *way* too many books about pirates.

PETER leans harder toward STAGE LEFT. If your puppet points, have him point STAGE LEFT.

DISCIPLE 1 perks up.

DISCIPLE 2 perks up.

DISCIPLE 2 looks to the sky and shakes his head "no."

DISCIPLE 1 peers STAGE LEFT.

PETER turns to DISCIPLE 1.

PETER turns back to STAGE LEFT and raises his hands to his mouth.

DISCIPLE 2 shakes his head "no" and speaks to DISCIPLE 1.

DISCIPLE 1 looks at DISCIPLE 2.

## DISCIPLE 1
(To DISCIPLE 2) Keep rowing. I'll keep bailing.

## PETER
(Calling) Wait! Look there!

## DISCIPLE 1
Is it a boat?

## DISCIPLE 2
Is it a shore?

## DISCIPLE 1
Is it a large, jagged pile of rocks growing ominously closer?

## DISCIPLE 2
*That* does it! I'm *swimming* for shore.

## DISCIPLE 1
(Awed) No, wait—it's a *man*...and he's walking on the water! And he's coming *this way*!

## PETER
(Amazed) I think it's Jesus. I can hear him!

(Calling) Lord, if it's you, tell me to come to you on the water!

## DISCIPLE 2
(Disbelieving) Is he nuts? You can't walk on water!

## DISCIPLE 1
(Confidently) Jesus is doing it.

DISCIPLE 2 is still talking to DISCIPLE 1.

## DISCIPLE 2
(Protesting) Well, yeah, but Jesus is *Jesus*. Peter is just...*Peter*! If Peter steps out of this boat, he's gonna sink like a rock.

## DISCIPLE 1
I don't think this is about who *you* are. I think it's about having faith in who *Jesus* is.

DISCIPLE 2 speaks to DISCIPLE 1.

## DISCIPLE 2
Yeah, whatever. I *still* say Peter's gonna be talkin' to fish.

PETER turns to DISCIPLE 2 and DISCIPLE 1.

## PETER
Jesus says to walk over to him.

## DISCIPLE 1
(Concerned) Are you sure that's a good idea? We could try rowing over...

PETER steps up and out of boat, which continues to bob in the high seas. PETER crosses and exits STAGE LEFT.

## PETER
Wait for me here.

DISCIPLE 1 and DISCIPLE 2 look STAGE LEFT.

## DISCIPLE 1
(Excitedly) He's *doing* it! Peter's walking on water!

## DISCIPLE 2
(Amazement shifting to cold observation) I can't believe it! Boy, if you'd told me I'd ever see someone walk on the...Wait a minute...

DISCIPLE 1 tries to look over DISCIPLE 2.

## DISCIPLE 1
What's happening?

## DISCIPLE 2

Peter's looking at the waves instead of looking at Jesus...Now he's starting to sink a little...

DISCIPLE 1 raises his hands to his mouth.

## DISCIPLE 1

(Calling, concerned) Peter! Keep your eyes on Jesus!

## DISCIPLE 2

Now he's *really* looking at the waves...and he's up to his *knees*...

## DISCIPLE 1

(Calling and concerned) Peter! Keep looking at Jesus!

## DISCIPLE 2

(As if doing a play-by-play sports show) Now he's up to his armpits and...and Jesus is reaching down and pulling Peter out.

## DISCIPLE 1

(Disappointed) I can't *believe* it! Peter was doing so well! He *knew* Jesus was there, he *knew* Jesus had the power to walk on water, and he *knew* Jesus told him to get out of the boat. What went wrong?

DISCIPLE 2 double takes the bottom of the boat and DISCIPLE 1.

## DISCIPLE 2

(Concerned) I vote we figure it out later. If we don't get moving, we'll need rescuing, too. This time *you* row and *I'll* bail.

DISCIPLE 2 and DISCIPLE 1 change places.

## DISCIPLE 1

OK.

## DISCIPLE 2

Let's go pick them up. Peter looks like he needs to sit down.

BOAT rows across stage and exits STAGE LEFT.

**Skit Eleven:**
*Peter on the Water*

77

## For Deeper Learning

Say: Peter did fine as long as he kept his eyes on Jesus. But when he looked at the crashing waves and thought about how deep the water was, he started to sink.

We're just like Peter. When we trust Jesus to take care of us, we're fine. When we stop looking to Jesus, we're sunk!

Have children form groups of three or four and discuss:

- Peter had just been with Jesus and had seen Jesus do miraculous things. Why do you think Peter didn't trust Jesus to care for him?

- Do you think Jesus can be trusted? Why or why not?

- Tell me about a time you forgot to trust Jesus.

# Grateful Leper

**Bible Reference:** Luke 17:11-19

## Cast

**DOCTOR:** nice adult male whose world is about to be rattled

**DAVID:** adult male who is very happy about being healed

## Costuming: Dress both the doctor and David in Bible-times costumes. The doctor's costume is white. Place a doctor's reflector around doctor's forehead.

## Props: Bible-times costumes, doctor's reflector (You can create a puppet-sized one with a canning lid.)

SCRIPT

| ACTIONS | WORDS |
|---|---|
|  *Play track 2 on CD B.* <br><br> DOCTOR quickly crosses to CENTER STAGE and addresses audience. | **DOCTOR** <br><br> **(Shouting)** Is there a doctor in the house? Is there a doctor in the house? <br><br> Are any of you doctors? Raise your hand if you've been to medical school. <br><br> **(2 SECOND PAUSE)** No, not *pre*school, *medical* school... <br><br> You can always spot a doctor because they usually wear white. And they usually have one of these shiny reflector things on their heads. And they're usually in a hurry. Wait a minute! *I'm* wearing white! *I've* got a shiny thing on my head! *I'm* in a hurry! *I'm* a doctor! <br><br> We doctors have lots of stuff to think about. Like who's sick, and who's healthy, and how we're gonna help. I think about that stuff even when I'm here in the marketplace. |

DAVID enters from STAGE LEFT and crosses toward STAGE RIGHT. He's humming to himself and walking with a happy jaunt. DAVID speaks to DOCTOR as he passes DOCTOR at CENTER STAGE.

**DAVID**
(Happily humming) Dum-de-de-dah-dum...Hiya, Doc!

DOCTOR looks at DAVID.

**DOCTOR**
Oh, hi, David. How's your leprosy doing?

DAVID continues to move.

**DAVID**
(Cheerfully) It's gone. I'm healthy as a mule now.

DOCTOR turns to look at David.

**DOCTOR**
Good for you. Like I was saying...

Hey, wait a minute! You can't be healthy! Leprosy doesn't just go away!

DAVID looks at DOCTOR.

**DAVID**
(Cheerfully) Mine did.

**DOCTOR**
That's *impossible*! There's...

(Calmly) Would you wait here a moment?

**DAVID**
(Cheerfully) Sure.

DOCTOR returns to FRONT CENTER STAGE and talks to audience.
DOCTOR looks out at the audience.

**DOCTOR**
(Calmly) Let me tell you about leprosy: First David's skin got a weird patch on it, and then blobs started growing on his face and body, and then his fingers and his toes got all bent. And there's no cure! So how could he be better?

DOCTOR returns to stand facing DAVID.

(Frantic again) Hey, how could you be *better*? There's no *cure*!

Skit Twelve:
*Grateful Leper*

| | |
|---|---|
| | **DAVID**<br>(Cheerfully) Well, maybe *you* couldn't cure me, but... |
| DOCTOR looks around secretly. | **DOCTOR**<br>(Speaking in hushed tones) And you know it's against the rules for people with leprosy to be here in the marketplace. If people find out that someone with leprosy is here, you'll be in a *world* of trouble! |
| DAVID bounces excitedly. | **DAVID**<br>(Celebrating loudly) But I'm healthy! *No more leprosy!* |
| DOCTOR looks at DAVID. | **DOCTOR**<br>Are you *crazy?* Everybody heard you! |
| DOCTOR turns to look at audience and around off both sides of stage to make sure people aren't looking. | (Loudly, with bad acting) Ha-ha! What a joke! No one here has leprosy! No, sir!<br><br>You gotta be more careful! You can't go around yelling "leprosy" in a crowded place! Calm down! |
| DAVID bounces excitedly again. | **DAVID**<br>(Gleefully) I can't help it! I feel like shouting! I'm healed! |
| DOCTOR bounces excitedly. | **DOCTOR**<br>(Building in intensity) David, *I* examined you. *I* told you the bad news! Trust me, *you have leprosy*! |
| DOCTOR looks around at the audience. | Oh, oh...I mean...(Loudly) He's not here! He *left*, you see!<br><br>(Relieved) Whew! That was close! |
| | **DAVID**<br>You want to know what happened? Why I'm all better? |

| Stage directions | Dialogue |
|---|---|
| DOCTOR looks at audience and back to DAVID. | **DOCTOR**<br>Absolutely! I mean, I see you, and you *look* healthy, but how could that happen? |
| DAVID looks from DOCTOR to audience. | **DAVID**<br>(Cheerfully) I was living out in the hills with other lepers, begging for food because I couldn't get a job. Then a few weeks ago, Jesus passed by on the road to Jerusalem. You know, that one that runs along the border between Samaria and Galilee. |
| | **DOCTOR**<br>Jesus? Isn't he the teacher? |
| DAVID raises both hands. | **DAVID**<br>Teacher *and* healer. Anyway, ten of us guys ran over and asked Jesus to heal us. He told us to go show ourselves to the priests. While we were going we were healed. |
| | **DOCTOR**<br>Just like that? No medicine? |
| DAVID starts to jiggle with joy as he speaks. | **DAVID**<br>Just like that. No medicine. And I'm all better! |
| DOCTOR shakes his head "no." | **DOCTOR**<br>No operation? |
| DAVID shakes his head "no." | **DAVID**<br>No operation! |
| DOCTOR shakes his head "no." | **DOCTOR**<br>You didn't even have to stick out your tongue? |
| DAVID shakes his head "no." | **DAVID**<br>Nope. Jesus *healed* us, just like that. I went back, fell at his feet, and said "thanks," but the other nine guys didn't |

Skit Twelve:
*Grateful Leper*

DOCTOR looks at DAVID then up to heaven.

bother. They ran straight home, I guess.

**DOCTOR**
So you once had leprosy and now...you're... *healed*! That's...that's...a *miracle*!

**DAVID**
That's what I thought.

**DOCTOR**
(Excitedly) Jesus healed David! Jesus healed David of leprosy!

DAVID tries to hush DOCTOR.

**DAVID**
(Hushing) Doctor, people will hear you saying the "L" word.

DOCTOR jumps with excitement.

**DOCTOR**
I don't care! I've just seen a miracle! (Yelling to the crowd) Jesus just healed David of leprosy! I thought he was going to die, and now he's perfectly fine! It was a miracle!

DOCTOR looks at DAVID.

Come on, David. We have to tell everyone about this miracle. We have to find the other nine guys so they can tell everyone too.

DAVID and DOCTOR exit STAGE RIGHT.

(Yelling from offstage) A miracle! I can't believe it, but I do believe. Jesus, I believe! Jesus, I believe, I believe!

## For Deeper Learning

Say: **Jesus is the best doctor ever! He can heal anyone without giving a shot.**

Have children form groups of three or four and discuss:

- **If you were the leper, how would you have felt when Jesus healed you?**
- **Why do you think Jesus decided to heal the leper and his nine friends?**
- **In what ways has Jesus helped you in your life?**

# Mary and Martha

**Bible Reference:** Luke 10:38-42

## Cast

**MARY:** adult female who is pleasant and open with her opinions

**MARTHA:** offstage adult female who is worried and hurried

**MIKE ROPHONE:** adult male television host who speaks with a TV voice

**NARRATOR:** offstage television announcer

## Costuming: Mary is in Bible-times costume. Mike has a Bible-times costume with a tie. Place a microphone in Mike's hand.

## Props: Bible-times costumes, tie, water spray bottle with a good range

---

SCRIPT

| ACTIONS | WORDS |
|---|---|
| *Play track 3 on CD B.* | **NARRATOR**<br>**(From offstage)** Welcome to the number one reality show in television prime time, *That's Your Choice*. And now here's your host, Mike Rophone... |
| MIKE enters from STAGE LEFT. | **MIKE**<br>Real stories, real choices, real people. Two sisters who live in the same house in Bethany. Two women who faced the same situation. Two women who made very different choices. Let's welcome Mary and her sister, Martha! |
| MARY enters from STAGE RIGHT. | **MARY**<br>Thank you. Thank you very much. |
| MIKE looks around. | **MIKE**<br>Thanks for joining us, Mary. I thought your sister, Martha, would also be here. |

MARY looks at MIKE.

MARY and MIKE follow sound from right to left.

MIKE looks at MARY.

MIKE looks at the audience and then back to MARY.

MARY and MIKE follow sound from left to right.
MARY looks at MIKE.

**MARY**
Oh, she's here. She's just running around taking care of things so fast it's sometimes hard to see her.

**MARTHA**
**(Calling offstage)** Watch out! Comin' through!

**MIKE**
**(Amazed)** She really *does* move fast! I didn't even see her go by!

**MARY**
You don't know the half of it. Always cooking, always cleaning, no matter what.

**MIKE**
And that brings us to what happened on the day in question, doesn't it? A day when you and Martha had to make a choice.

**MARY**
You're talking about the day Jesus and his disciples came to eat, right?

**MIKE**
Tell us about that fateful afternoon...

**MARTHA**
**(Calling from offstage)** Laundry to do!

**MARY**
Well, of course Jesus and his disciples coming to eat was a *very* big deal to us. We wanted the house to be clean from top to bottom and to prepare the best meal we knew how to make...

**Skit Thirteen:**
*Mary and Martha*

MIKE looks at MARY.

**MIKE**
And yet that's not what happened, is it? That day the unexpected occurred…

**MARY**
Now I think cleaning is important, but Martha was *very* worried about plumping the cushions and getting the meal just right. She really *cares* about the details…

**MARTHA**
**(Calling from offstage)** Dusting! Outta the way!

MARY and MIKE follow sound from right to left.

**MIKE**
**(Out of character, amazed)** Does she *always* do that? How do you keep from getting run over?

MIKE shakes his head in disbelief.

**MARY**
You get used to it. Anyway, we'd been cleaning and cooking a long time when Jesus and his disciples came to our door. It was so good to see Jesus, but we just weren't ready yet. I hadn't set the table, and Martha was right in the middle of changing the shelf paper in the pantry…

MARY shrugs and lifts her arms.

**MIKE**
Jesus is a friend of yours?

**MARY**
A friend? He's my *best* friend! When I met Jesus, my life changed completely! Well, you've seen Martha. She hardly stopped to say, "Hi!" She kept cooking and cleaning and dashing about.

MARY nods her head "yes."

**MIKE**
So even as Jesus and his disciples were sitting in the living room…

**Skit Thirteen:**
**Mary and Martha**

| Stage Directions | Dialogue |
|---|---|
| MARY and MIKE follow sound from left to right. | **MARTHA**<br>**(Calling from offstage)** Lunch is served! |
| MARY looks at MIKE. | **MARY**<br>Martha just kept moving faster and faster, *determined* to finish cleaning. But I just wanted to be with Jesus. So I plopped myself down near him and listened as he taught his disciples. |
| MIKE looks at MARY. | **MIKE**<br>How did Martha take that? |
| MARY raises her hands in disbelief. | **MARY**<br>**(With a bit of attitude)** She got angry! She told Jesus to order me back to the kitchen so I could help finish preparing the meal! |
| MARY lowers her arms. | **(Calmer)** But I wanted to listen to *Jesus*. He was in our house, and Martha was so busy making the house perfect for him that she almost *missed* him! |
| | **MIKE**<br>And what did Jesus say? |
| MARY looks out at the audience. | **MARY**<br>He *agreed* with me! I'm sure he and Peter and the bunch were looking forward to one of Martha's home-cooked meals—she makes the best barbecued lamb chops—but Jesus said I made the best choice when I decided to be with him instead of out in the kitchen. Jesus wants us to be with him instead of just doing good things all the time. |
| | **MIKE**<br>Well, well, well. That must have slowed Martha down a bit. |

**Skit Thirteen:**
Mary and Martha

MARY looks back at MIKE.


MARY and MIKE follow sound from right to left.
MIKE looks back at MARY.












MARY and MIKE continue to talk with each other.




From behind the set, a spray of water goes up over the puppets and lands on audience.

**MARY**
For a while it did, but old habits are hard to break. She's been zipping around ever since...

**MARTHA**
(**Calling from offstage**) Dishes to wash!

**MIKE**
I see what you mean.

**MARY**
We have to make choices every day. My choice is to be with Jesus every chance I get, even if the pot roast overcooks.

**MIKE**
Mary, thanks for joining us. And Martha—if you can hear this—thanks for *almost* joining us. Two women, two choices, and the choice that pleased Jesus was the choice to be with him.

So remember, no matter where you go or what you do, it's your life, and you have choices to make. Join us next week on *That's Your Choice*!

I wish we could have gotten a word with your sister, Martha...

**MARY**
That would have been nice. You're just lucky she didn't notice that the audience needed a good washing and waxing. She'd have been...

**MARTHA**
(**Calling from offstage**) Dusty audience! We can't have a dusty audience!

MARY turns to audience.

**MARY**
**(Calling)** Everyone duck your heads! She's gonna wash you!

**MIKE**
**(Yelling)** I'm out of here—I didn't take a shower today!

MARY dashes off STAGE RIGHT.

**MARY**
**(Calling)** Martha! Leave him alone! Martha!

## For Deeper Learning

Say: **Whew! Martha is *serious* about cleaning! But if it comes down to a choice between a clean house and a clean heart, the clean heart wins. And if it's a choice between being with Jesus and cleaning house, being with Jesus wins.**

**Martha isn't the only one who sometimes makes poor choices.**

Have children form small groups of three or four and discuss:

- **Why do you think Martha thought she was making a good choice?**
- **What can you learn from Martha and Mary's story?**
- **What's a choice you need to make in the coming week? How can you make sure what you decide is the best choice?**

# Lazarus

**Bible Reference:** John 11:1–12:2

**Cast**

> **BERNIE:** excitable adult male businessman with questionable ethics
>
> **LAZARUS:** even-tempered adult male

**Costuming:** Dress Bernie and Lazarus in Bible-times costumes.

**Props:** Bible-times costumes, sign that reads: "Bernie's Fine Funerals"

**Setup:** Before the skit begins, place the "Bernie's Fine Funerals" sign near stage left.

## SCRIPT

| ACTIONS | WORDS |
|---|---|
| 💿 *Play track 4 on CD B.* | |
| BERNIE stands by sign, STAGE LEFT, singing to himself. | **BERNIE**<br>Dum, dum, dum...It's always so boring this time of year. |
| BERNIE turns to the audience and addresses the audience. | Everybody healthy, no business for me...dum, de dum...Say, do all of you people feel healthy? Stick out your tongues. Let me hear you say "ah." Louder! **(2 second pause)**<br><br>Hmmm...rats. I think you're all gonna make it. Oh, well...dum, de, dum, de dum dum dum... |
| LAZARUS enters STAGE RIGHT. | **BERNIE**<br>Hi, can I help you? |
| BERNIE and LAZARUS look at each other. | **LAZARUS**<br>I came to talk about a funeral. |

| | |
|---|---|
| BERNIE straightens up and moves toward LAZARUS. | **BERNIE**<br>(Cheerful) Well, you're in the right place. Bernie's Fine Funerals, that's us. I'm Bernie. And you are…? |
| | **LAZARUS**<br>Lazarus. |
| BERNIE looks from LAZARUS to audience and back to LAZARUS. BERNIE scratches his head. | **BERNIE**<br>(Thinking) Lazarus. Hmmm…I've heard that name lately. Say, you aren't the guy who won the big chariot race, are you? |
| LAZARUS shakes his head "no." | **LAZARUS**<br>No, not me. |
| BERNIE still scratches his head. | **BERNIE**<br>Too bad—I was going to get an autograph. |
| | **LAZARUS**<br>Actually, I'm… |
| BERNIE stops scratching his head and holds up his hand to stop LAZARUS. | **BERNIE**<br>(Interrupting, confident) No, no—don't tell me. I'll get it. I never forget a name or a face. |
| | **LAZARUS**<br>(Bemused) You seem to be forgetting *mine*. |
| BERNIE shakes his head as if he still doesn't remember. | **BERNIE**<br>Are you sure we've met? |
| LAZARUS nods his head "yes" to the audience and then looks at BERNIE. | **LAZARUS**<br>(Ironic) *Oh*, yeah, we've met. |
| | **BERNIE**<br>Give me a hint. |

**Skit Fourteen:**
Lazarus

BERNIE leans toward LAZARUS.

**LAZARUS**
(Flatly) I want my money back.

**BERNIE**
*That's* my hint?

LAZARUS nods his head "yes."

**LAZARUS**
Yup.

**BERNIE**
(Befuddled) You want your money back for *what*?

LAZARUS holds his hands out to his side as if for inspection.

**LAZARUS**
My funeral. You buried me two weeks ago.

BERNIE speaks and then his mouth drops open.

**BERNIE**
(Stunned) You're *that* Lazarus? What are you doing walking around? You were *dead*! We *buried* you!

**LAZARUS**
I know. But it turns out I didn't need the funeral after all, so...

BERNIE shakes his head "no."

**BERNIE**
(Protesting) You can't ask for your money back after we put you in a tomb! When we bury someone, they're supposed to *stay* buried! What went wrong?

LAZARUS drops his arms.

**LAZARUS**
You mean what went wrong with my funeral?

BERNIE nods his head "yes" and then turns to the audience and then back to LAZARUS.

**BERNIE**
Yes! If everything went *right*, you'd still be dead!

**LAZARUS**
I don't see it quite that way, but I guess I can explain. See, when I was sick, my sisters, Mary and Martha, sent a message asking Jesus to come and heal me.

Both of BERNIE'S hands go to his head.

**BERNIE**
(Curious) Can Jesus *do* that?

LAZARUS nods his head "yes."

**LAZARUS**
Oh, yeah, no problem.

BERNIE turns to the audience.

**BERNIE**
(Thoughtfully) *That* could be bad for my business...

BERNIE turns to LAZARUS.

(Pushing) Go on, then what happened?

**LAZARUS**
Jesus didn't leave to come see me for a while, and by the time he got here, I'd been dead and buried for four days.

**BERNIE**
Right. It was a *very* nice service, by the way.

LAZARUS looks from BERNIE to audience.

**LAZARUS**
My sisters told me, thanks. Anyway, Jesus told my sisters that he was the Resurrection and the Life, and whoever believes in him would live even though he died. Martha told Jesus she believed he was the Son of God, and then my sisters took him out to where I was buried.

BERNIE looks up as if remembering and then nods his head "yes."

**BERNIE**
A first-class tomb, too. Nice cave, very heavy rock in front of it. Classy.

**LAZARUS**
I know. I was there. So Jesus had some guys move the rock, and he said, "Lazarus, come out." And I did. Good as new. And that's why my sisters want their money back.

BERNIE tilts his head to the left.

**BERNIE**
Let me get this straight: Jesus raised you from the dead.

**LAZARUS**
Right.

**BERNIE**
And Jesus is the Son of God.

LAZARUS nods his head "yes."

**LAZARUS**
Right.

**BERNIE**
And Jesus can raise anyone he wants to from the dead, any time, any place.

BERNIE looks around so no one else will hear.

And Jesus is planning to do this a *lot* around here?

LAZARUS looks around, imitating BERNIE'S moves.

**LAZARUS**
Well, he didn't say anything about it specifically...

BERNIE relaxes.

**BERNIE**
Good, I can't have everyone coming in here looking for refunds!

**LAZARUS**
So what about the money?

BERNIE straightens himself and faces LAZARUS.

**BERNIE**
(Resolutely) Sorry, but we did our part. A deal is a deal. I suppose I *could* give you a

LAZARUS shakes his head "no."

BERNIE looks around nervously.

LAZARUS shakes his head "no."

LAZARUS exits STAGE RIGHT.

BERNIE exits STAGE RIGHT.

credit for next time in case you plan to die again sometime soon.

## LAZARUS
Boy, I hope not. I'd rather have the cash.

## BERNIE
(Resolute, pushy) Then you're out of luck. In this business it's all deposit, no return. Now take off! We're closed. It's time for lunch. We're doing inventory. I called in sick.

## LAZARUS
(Mumbling to self) *This* isn't very good service...

## BERNIE
I gotta lock up before Jesus raises someone else! This could *ruin* me!

## For Deeper Learning

Say: **What a surprise for Lazarus' friends and family—Jesus raised him from the dead!** *That's* **not something that happens every day!**

**Except it will happen for you, too, if you trust in Jesus and follow him. The Bible says in 1 Corinthians 15 that even if you die on earth, you'll get a new body that will last forever in heaven. What a great thing!**

Have children form groups of three or four and discuss:

- **If you were a friend of Lazarus, how would you have felt seeing him alive again?**

- **If you were a friend of Lazarus, how would you have felt about Jesus after Jesus raised your friend?**

- **How do you feel about living forever in heaven with Jesus?**

# Prodigal Son

**Bible Reference:** Luke 15:11-32

## Cast

**DIRECTOR:** kind but businesslike adult male

**BRUCE:** beginning adult male actor who's nervous

**DAPHNE:** adult female who is a seasoned stage voice

**FRANKIE:** adult male with a New Jersey accent who is working every angle

## Costuming: None of the puppets wear Bible-times costumes.

## Props: None

SCRIPT

| ACTIONS | WORDS |
|---|---|
| *Play track 5 on CD B.* | |
| DIRECTOR enters from STAGE RIGHT and addresses audience. | **DIRECTOR**<br>Ladies and gentlemen, thank you for coming to the auditions for our new play, *The Prodigal Son*. I asked any actors who wanted to play the part of a pig to stop by to try out. I'd like you to help me decide who gets the part, OK? **(Pause.)** After everyone tries out, we'll vote to see who gets the part. Let's get started.<br><br>**(Calling)** Send in the first actor! |
| BRUCE enters STAGE LEFT, crosses to CENTER STAGE.<br>BRUCE nods his head "yes." | Your name is Bruce, right?<br><br>**BRUCE**<br>Yes, sir.<br><br>**DIRECTOR**<br>Let's see what you've got. Pretend you're a pig. |

| | |
|---|---|
| BRUCE looks up as if he's thinking. | **BRUCE**<br>Before I begin, could you tell me a little more about the role? What's my motivation? |
| DIRECTOR looks at BRUCE. | **DIRECTOR**<br>You're a pig. I'm not sure you *have* a motivation. |
| BRUCE raises his hands. | **BRUCE**<br>Can't you tell me *anything*? |
| DIRECTOR wanders around stage expressively as he shares story. | **DIRECTOR**<br>(Amicably) Sure. The play tells a story first told by Jesus. It's about a young man who has a rich father. The kid can't *wait* to collect his inheritance—the money given to a son when his father dies. So he asks his dad for the money early. Then he goes off and spends it on parties in a distant land. |
| | **BRUCE**<br>Where does the pig come in? |
| DIRECTOR motions for patience. | **DIRECTOR**<br>I'm getting to that. See, the kid runs out of money, and once he's poor, his friends all leave. So the kid takes a job caring for pigs. He's so hungry that he eats what the pigs eat. Then he decides to go home and beg his dad for a job. |
| | **BRUCE**<br>Does he take the pigs with him? |
| DIRECTOR shakes his head "no." | **DIRECTOR**<br>No. The pigs stay behind. And when the father sees his son walking up the road, the father runs to the son and welcomes him home. |

BRUCE double takes the audience and DIRECTOR.

BRUCE holds hand to chin as he is taking it all in.

DIRECTOR returns to STAGE RIGHT.

DIRECTOR double takes the audience and BRUCE.

BRUCE scoops his head to deliver his line.

DIRECTOR slowly shakes his head.

BRUCE becomes animated again.

DIRECTOR drops his head so as to not look BRUCE in the face.

BRUCE exits STAGE RIGHT as DAPHNE enters STAGE LEFT and crosses to CENTER STAGE.

**BRUCE**
The father wasn't mad?

**DIRECTOR**
The father was forgiving. He even threw a party for his son.

**BRUCE**
(Thoughtfully) I see. It's a great story.

**DIRECTOR**
I know. When people heard Jesus tell it, they were able to see how much God loves them. We want people to feel the same way when they see our play. So let's see if you can help us. Show me how you'd play the part of a pig.

**BRUCE**
(Clears throat, then delivers a deadpan line) Ahem...oink.

**DIRECTOR**
Oink? That's it?

**BRUCE**
(Deadpan) Oink-*oink*.

**DIRECTOR**
Gee...well...thanks so much for coming in...

**BRUCE**
(Eagerly) Do you think I'll get the part?

**DIRECTOR**
(Rushing) Can't really say, Bruce. Got some other people coming in to audition, but if you'll leave your name and number on the sheet by the door, we'll be in touch.

(Calling) Next!

DAPHNE moves deliberately and slowly.

**DAPHNE**
(Speaking lyrically and directly) Hello. I'm Daphne, and I've played the part of a pig before—twice.

DIRECTOR looks up from being busy.

**DIRECTOR**
(Pleasantly surprised) Really? That's great. We don't get a lot of people with experience playing this particular role. Tell me about it.

**DAPHNE**
I was in a bacon commercial, and I played the part of the fifth slice of bacon from the left.

**DIRECTOR**
How do you...*do* that exactly?

As DAPHNE delivers impersonation, she shakes all over.

**DAPHNE**
Well, I was in a frying pan, and so it went something like this...

(Impersonating sizzling grease)
Ssssssssssssssssszzzzzzzzz.

DIRECTOR slowly looks at audience and then back to DAPHNE.

**DIRECTOR**
Actually, we're looking for *uncooked* pigs. It's for Jesus' story of the prodigal son. Are you familiar with it?

DAPHNE nods her head "yes."

**DAPHNE**
Of course. Very.

**DIRECTOR**
Then let's hear you do a pig. A non-frying one.

**DAPHNE**
I shall reprise my role of Anita, from the all-pork production of *The Smell of Swine*. Ahem...

DAPHNE overplays the role, moving dramatically.

(Singing—approximately, NOT exactly—to the tune of "The hills are alive with the sound of music," title line only) Oink, oink, oink, oink, oink; oink, oink, oink, oink, oink, oink.

**DIRECTOR**
Um...what *was* that exactly?

**DAPHNE**
I'm *a singing* pig.

DIRECTOR shakes as if he were on the edge of losing his temper.

**DIRECTOR**
This isn't a musical. We don't need a singing pig. No frying, no singing. Leave your name and number at the door, please.

(Calling) Next!

FRANKIE enters from STAGE LEFT as DAPHNE exits STAGE RIGHT.

**FRANKIE**
How ya doin'?

DIRECTOR looks down as if examining paper work.

**DIRECTOR**
Fine. You're here to try out for the role of the pig?

FRANKIE shakes his head "no."

**FRANKIE**
No. I'm Frankie DeMatta and I'm here because my partner, who is poifect for the part, is tryin' out.

DIRECTOR looks up at FRANKIE.

**DIRECTOR**
Where's your partner?

FRANKIE points STAGE LEFT. Both DIRECTOR and FRANKIE walk STAGE LEFT and look.

**FRANKIE**
Out in da lobby dere. See?

DIRECTOR slowly turns his head and looks at FRANKIE.

**DIRECTOR**
Your partner is a *dog*?

| | |
|---|---|
| FRANKIE looks STAGE LEFT. | **FRANKIE**<br>Yeah, but not just *any* dog. That is Geraldo, the *Wonder* Dog. Smartest dog in the world!<br><br>(Calling) Ain't that right, Geraldo?<br><br>**GERALDO**<br>(From offstage) Ruff!<br><br>**FRANKIE**<br>(Self-satisfied) See?<br><br>**DIRECTOR**<br>That doesn't prove anything.<br><br>**FRANKIE**<br>A doubter, huh? Watch this. |
| Calling STAGE LEFT. | Hey, Geraldo, what's that thing what sits on top of a house?<br><br>(From offstage) Ruff!<br><br>**FRANKIE**<br>A roof—exactly! |
| Calling STAGE LEFT. | Hey, Geraldo, what's the opposite of smooth?<br><br>**GERALDO**<br>(From offstage) Ruff! |
| DIRECTOR drops his head. | **FRANKIE**<br>(Smugly) Correctamundo. Rough. The opposite of smooth is rough. |
| DIRECTOR raises his head to look at FRANKIE. | **DIRECTOR**<br>(Protesting) But all he's doing is... |

**Skit Fifteen:**
*Prodigal Son*

Calling STAGE LEFT.



DIRECTOR crosses to CENTER STAGE;
FRANKIE follows.



Calling STAGE LEFT.

FRANKIE and DIRECTOR look stage left,
then at each other as level drops.

**FRANKIE**
One more!

Hey, Geraldo, who's the greatest baseball
player who ever played the game?

**GERALDO**
(From offstage) Ruff!

**FRANKIE**
One more!

(Smugly) Babe Ruth. Right again. Three
for three. See what I mean?

**DIRECTOR**
Even if he's smart, I don't *need* a dog. I
need a *pig*!

**FRANKIE**
No problem! He does impersonations.

Hey, Geraldo, pretend you're a pig!

**DIRECTOR**
(Admiringly) He's good. *Really* good.

**FRANKIE**
(Self-satisfied) So he gets the part, right?

**DIRECTOR**
That depends. What do we have to pay
him?

**FRANKIE**
(Dismissively) You're in luck; he works
cheap. See, Geraldo ran away from home
a couple months ago, and when he came

slinkin' back with his tail tucked between his legs, I welcomed him home with open arms. Gave him a bath, fed him some food, took care of him. He's just glad to be home, so if I ask him he'll do the part for...oh, six boxes of doggie treats and a rawhide bone.

## DIRECTOR
Two boxes of treats.

## FRANKIE
*Three* boxes of treats *and* a chew toy and we got a deal.

## DIRECTOR
(**To audience**) I know I said we'd vote, but we can't pass up a deal like *this*.

Geraldo's got the job.

## FRANKIE
(**Enthusiastically**) Hey, you won't be sorry! Let's go give him the good news.

## DIRECTOR
And get him out of the lobby, will you? He's confusing everyone.

## FRANKIE
No problem. Hey, Geraldo, knock it off!

I said he was smart. I never said he was polite.

DIRECTOR turns to audience.


To FRANKIE.




FRANKIE and DIRECTOR move to STAGE LEFT.


Calling STAGE LEFT.

FRANKIE turns toward DIRECTOR.

FRANKIE and DIRECTOR exit.

Skit Fifteen:
*Prodigal Son*

## For Deeper Learning

Say: **Both the prodigal son and Geraldo had something in common. Can anyone tell me what that is?** Wait for responses. **They both ran away. When they came back, they were welcomed home. When Jesus told the story of the prodigal son, he wasn't talking about just the son. He was** *also* **talking about the father.**

**God is like that father who forgave his son when the young man came home and asked for forgiveness. God will forgive us when we come to him, too!**

Have children form groups of three or four and discuss:

- Have you ever forgiven someone? Tell about what happened.

- Have you ever done something wrong and someone forgave you? How did that feel? Why?

- Have you asked God to forgive you for your sins—those things you've done that were wrong? How did that feel?

# Little Girl on His Lap

**Bible Reference:** Matthew 19:13-15

## Cast

**DISCIPLE 7:** adult male who is very "Secret Service"

**FATHER 1:** nice adult male who has problems being assertive

**FATHER 2:** adult male who has no problems being assertive

**LITTLE GIRL:** female child with a cute voice but willing to speak her mind

**NARRATOR:** offstage voice who sets the stage

## Costuming: All characters wear Bible-times costumes.
Disciple 7 wears a dark robe and sunglasses.

## Props: Bible-times costumes, dark robe, sunglasses on Disciple 7

---

### SCRIPT

| ACTIONS | WORDS |
|---|---|
|  *Play track 6 on CD B.* | |
| During the NARRATOR'S voice-over DISCIPLE 7 has entered STAGE LEFT and crossed to CENTER STAGE. He stands facing STAGE RIGHT. | **NARRATOR**<br>**(Offstage)** Jesus left Galilee and went into the region of Judah. Large crowds followed him. Then little children were brought to Jesus for him to place his hands on them and pray for them. But the disciples rebuked those who brought children… |
| | **DISCIPLE 7**<br>**(Seriously)** Disciple 7 is in position. The eastern perimeter is secure.<br><br>Will do. Over and out. |
| FATHER 1 enters STAGE RIGHT and crosses to DISCIPLE 7. | **FATHER 1**<br>**(Amiably)** Hi! You're with Jesus, right? |

DISCIPLE 7 stays stiff and looks at the father only long enough to affirm that he's not a threat.

FATHER 1 still watches DISCIPLE 7.

DISCIPLE 7 continues to survey the area for trouble.

FATHER 1 turns to leave.

FATHER 1 raises hand to DISCIPLE 7 as if to say "wait."

Indicates STAGE RIGHT.

DISCIPLE 7 stops looking around and focuses on FATHER 1.

FATHER 1 drops hand and looks at DISCIPLE 7.

DISCIPLE 7 raises hand to move FATHER 1 along and out of his way.

FATHER 1 raises his hands to plead with DISCIPLE 7.

**DISCIPLE 7**
Affirmative.

**FATHER 1**
So if I wanted to talk with Jesus, you could help me do that?

**DISCIPLE 7**
Affirmative, can do.

**FATHER 1**
Great! I'm gonna go get my little boy and I'll be right back...

**DISCIPLE 7**
Negative, no can do. Jesus won't be seeing children today.

**FATHER 1**
But I'll be right back. He's right over there...

**DISCIPLE 7**
Doesn't matter. Jesus *won't* be seeing children today.

**FATHER 1**
(Concerned) But my son has been sick. The doctors have tried everything and nothing has worked. I just know if Jesus could pray for my little guy, he'd be healed.

**DISCIPLE 7**
Move along, please. Don't force me to take action.

**FATHER 1**
(Pleading) Please, mister—just two minutes with Jesus. A *minute*, even!

**Skit Sixteen:**
Little Girl on His Lap

FATHER 1 drops his head and his hands, then turns and leaves.

FATHER 1 exits STAGE RIGHT.

FATHER 2 and LITTLE GIRL enter from STAGE LEFT. DISCIPLE 7 turns and faces them.

FATHER 2 looks at DISCIPLE 7 and gestures toward his little girl.

FATHER 2 indicates STAGE LEFT.

FATHER 2 looks around in surprise.

## DISCIPLE 7
Base, come in, base.

We've got a situation here on the eastern perimeter. Send backup at once.

I'd move along now if I were you.

## FATHER 1
I'm leaving, I'm leaving...but you should be ashamed of yourself!

## DISCIPLE 7
(Accusingly) You two! How did you get through the lines?

## FATHER 2
What lines? It's just me and my little girl here.

## DISCIPLE 7
Exactly! No children can interrupt Jesus! He's much too busy to see children!

## FATHER 2
(Explaining) But Anna and I just met Jesus...right over there.

## DISCIPLE 7
(Angry) Someone is gonna be in big trouble for this! Big, *big* trouble! Who let you through? Was it Peter? He's always a sucker for a cute little face!

## FATHER 2
I don't understand...

## DISCIPLE 7
I'll explain it to you: Jesus does *not* have time to be interrupted by children. Is *that* plain enough for you? He's the Son of God!

He's talking about important things! He doesn't have time to kiss babies and let a bunch of little munchkins climb up on his lap!

LITTLE GIRL looks up at DISCIPLE 7.

**LITTLE GIRL**
You're a *mean* man!

FATHER 2 looks down at the LITTLE GIRL.

**FATHER 2**
**(Quietly, to Little Girl)** Hold your tongue, dear. Let me talk to the man.

FATHER 2 looks back to DISCIPLE 7.

My daughter has a point: You *are* a mean man. At least, you're a man who's making a mistake.

DISCIPLE 7 strikes his stiff stance again.

**DISCIPLE 7**
**(Sarcastically)** You think so?

FATHER 2 straightens himself and stands taller.

**FATHER 2**
**(Rising to the challenge)** Yeah, I *do* think so. Go ask Jesus. *He's* the one who said to let the little children come to him because the kingdom of heaven belongs to such as them.

**DISCIPLE 7**
**(Sarcastically)** When did Jesus ever say *that*?

FATHER 2 points STAGE LEFT.

**FATHER 2**
About five minutes ago, right over there. While he was looking at my daughter!

**DISCIPLE 7**
**(Uncertainly)** Really?

FATHER 2 stands even taller.

**FATHER 2**
It seems some of his disciples have been keeping children away from Jesus. Isn't that right?

**Skit Sixteen:**
*Little Girl on His Lap*

| | |
|---|---|
| DISCIPLE 7 shrinks a little. | **DISCIPLE 7**<br>**(Apologetically)** Well, it seemed like a good idea at the time. After all, he *is* busy. You can see that for yourself. We figured he might as well spend his time with grown-ups who can understand what he's saying. |
| FATHER 2 looks at LITTLE GIRL. | **FATHER 2**<br>Oh, little ones like Anna understand well enough. She understands that Jesus loves her. Isn't that what Jesus wants everyone to understand? |
| | **DISCIPLE 7**<br>Well, in a manner of *speaking...* |
| | **FATHER 2**<br>And she understands that you're being mean when you keep people away from Jesus. |
| DISCIPLE 7 shrinks a little more. | **DISCIPLE 7**<br>I suppose you *could* say that... |
| | **FATHER 2**<br>And she understands something else, too. Go ahead and tell him, honey. |
| LITTLE GIRL moves to front and looks at DISCIPLE 7. | **LITTLE GIRL**<br>**(Telling Disciple 7 off)** Your mommy should *spank* you! Go to your room! |
| | **DISCIPLE 7**<br>Well, if you say so...I was just trying to do my job... |
| LITTLE GIRL points her finger at DISCIPLE 7. | **LITTLE GIRL**<br>You need a timeout! |

DISCIPLE 7 shakes his head in agreement, then drops it in shame.

DISCIPLE 7 exits STAGE LEFT as LITTLE GIRL and FATHER 2 exit STAGE RIGHT.

**DISCIPLE 7**
Yes, ma'am...I'm on my way...

### For Deeper Learning

Say: **Imagine someone saying that children don't matter to Jesus! Children matter very much to Jesus. He always has time for people who want to be with him, no matter how young those people are.**

Have children form groups of three or four and discuss:

- **How does it feel knowing you're important to Jesus, the Son of God?**

- **If you could tell Jesus just one thing, what would it be?**

- **Who's someone you can tell about how important that person is to Jesus?**

**Skit Sixteen:**
Little Girl on His Lap

# Zaccheus

**Bible Reference:** Luke 19:1-9

## Cast

MAN: nice male adult who wants to be helpful

EMT 1: male or female who takes self very seriously

EMT 2: male or female who takes self very seriously

ZACCHAEUS: adult male who is a redeemed businessman

## Costuming: Man and Zacchaeus wear Bible-times costumes.

## Props: Bible-times costumes

## Setup: For this skit you'll need to create two simple towel puppets to act as the two EMTs. Simply tie a white hand towel over your fist as shown in the diagram. Draw on two eyes and a nose.

**SCRIPT**

| ACTIONS | WORDS |
|---|---|
|  *Play track 7 on CD B.*<br><br>MAN comes onto stage from STAGE RIGHT, moves to CENTER STAGE and addresses the audience. | **MAN**<br>Excuse me, your attention please...Thank you.<br><br>The management of this facility has asked me to make the following statement: The puppet show you are about to see refers to short people as "wee" people. The writers, producers, and performers do not wish in any way to offend any of you in our audience who might be short people yourselves. In fact, everyone stand up for a moment and let me get a good look at you. Everyone stand up, please... **(3 beats)**<br><br>Great, you're all huge, so you won't be offended. Except for you there in the back. Will you stand up? Oh, you are |

MAN exits STAGE RIGHT.

MAN jogs back on stage, huffing and puffing.

EMT 1 and EMT 2 rush on stage from STAGE RIGHT. They look around, then turn to MAN.

EMTs always wiggle a bit when they talk since they don't have mouths.

MAN examines the EMTs.

EMTs look at each other and then back to MAN.

standing up. Hah! That was just a little joke. Get it? "Little" joke?

Ahem...

Thank you for your understanding. Ladies and gentlemen, please take your seats again. Our show is about to begin.

## MAN
(Breathless) Whew! If jogging is so good for you, how come my lungs are about to explode? I gotta rest before I have a heart attack...

## EMT 1
(From offstage) OK, people, keep moving...

## EMT 2
(From offstage) Nothing for you to see here. Let us work...

## EMT 1
(Sternly) You there, civilian!

## EMT 2
(Sternly) We're EMTs, and we need your help!

## MAN
EMTs?

## EMT 1
(Sternly) Emergency Medical Towels. We're here on a fourteen-twenty-eight-six call.

## MAN
If that's about me saying I was gonna have a heart attack, I wasn't serious. And you guys are *quick*.

Skit Seventeen:
*Zacchaeus*

## EMT 1

(Sternly) A heart attack is a twenty-one-oh-four. We don't care about that. We're on a fourteen-twenty-eight-six.

## EMT 2

(Sternly) Right. Wee little man stuck in a sycamore tree. One Zacchaeus by name.

## MAN

Oh.

## EMT 1

(Sternly) Any sycamore trees around here, civilian?

MAN indicates STAGE LEFT.

## MAN

Well, that big tree over there...

That's a sycamore. But I don't see anyone stuck in it.

## EMT 1

(Sternly) Please refrain from offering medical opinions, civilian.

## EMT 2

(Sternly) Right. *We're* the Emergency Medical Towels.

## EMT 1

(Sternly) We don't see anyone stuck in that tree.

Both turn and look off STAGE LEFT, then look at MAN.

## MAN

Maybe he climbed down. When did you get the call?

## EMT 1

(Sternly) Two days ago. We got here as fast as we could.

MAN raises his hands to shrug.

**EMT 2**
(Sternly) We were in the laundry.

**MAN**
Well, if there's no one in the tree, maybe there's no emergency.

**EMT 1**
(Sternly) Or...it could be a fourteen-twenty-eight-*seven* situation, not a fourteen-twenty-eight-six.

EMTs look at each other.

**EMT 2**
(Sternly) Right, an *invisible* wee little man in a sycamore tree!

**EMT 1**
(Sternly) We have to get him down!

**EMT 2**
(Sternly) And right away!

Both turn and look off STAGE LEFT, then look at MAN.

**EMT 1**
(Sternly) We don't know how to get invisible wee little men out of sycamore trees.

**EMT 2**
(Sternly) Especially *tall* sycamore trees.

**MAN**
My *cat* was stuck up a tree once...

**EMT 1**
(Sternly) That's a fourteen-twenty-eight-*two* call—not the same thing.

**EMT 2**
(Sternly) Nope, not the same thing at all.

Skit Seventeen:
*Zacchaeus*

**MAN**
(Apologetically) Sorry. I was just trying to help...

**EMT 2**
(Sternly) Hey, I have an idea! Let's throw rocks until we knock him *out* of the tree. Then we don't have to climb it.

**EMT 1**
(Sternly) No can do. Then we'll have a twelve-twelve-sixty-one.

**EMT 2**
(Sternly) Oh, right...invisible wee little man with serious head injury...How about we throw him a rope, he ties it to himself, and we *pull* him out of the tree?

**EMT 1**
(Sternly) We don't have a rope that long.

**EMT 2**
(Sternly) Oh, right.

**EMT 1**
(Sternly) I've got it! We cut the *tree* down, and he'll come down *with* it!

**EMT 2**
(Sternly) Good idea! Let's go!

**MAN**
Well, *that* was certainly odd...

**ZACCHAEUS**
(Interested) What's going on?

**MAN**
They're trying to rescue an invisible guy who's stuck in that tree.

EMT 1 and EMT 2 rush off STAGE LEFT.

MAN looking STAGE LEFT and scratching his head.

ZACCHAEUS wanders on stage and joins MAN looking STAGE LEFT.

MAN points off STAGE LEFT.

**ZACCHAEUS**

Really? I was up there a couple days ago, and I didn't see anybody.

**MAN**

Of course you didn't see anybody. He's *invisible*. Besides...say, what's your name?

**ZACCHAEUS**

Zacchaeus.

**MAN**

Zacchaeus? *You're* the guy they're trying to rescue!

**EMT 1**

(Sternly from offstage) Timber!

**MAN**

(Calling) Hey, you don't have to keep looking! Zacchaeus isn't in that tree!

**EMT 1**

(Sternly from offstage) Of *course* he's not in this tree. We just looked!

**EMT 2**

(Sternly from offstage) Maybe he's in *another* sycamore tree. There's one over there.

**EMT 1**

(Sternly from offstage) Let's cut it down!

**MAN**

So you're Zacchaeus? I thought you'd be..."wee-er."

**ZACCHAEUS**

I've been working out.

MAN turns to ZACCHAEUS.

MAN does double take.

MAN yells toward STAGE LEFT.

Skit Seventeen:
*Zacchaeus*

| | |
|---|---|
| MAN nods his head "yes" to confirm that he understands. | **MAN**<br>So what were you doing up in a tree? If you don't mind me asking. |
| ZACCHAEUS points STAGE LEFT. | **ZACCHAEUS**<br>I climbed up so i could see Jesus. He came right by here, on this road. There was a big crowd and being sort of...well, a little on the... |
| | **MAN**<br>Wee side? |
| ZACCHAEUS nods his head in agreement. | **ZACCHAEUS**<br>Yeah, that. Being a little on the wee side, I figured I'd see better from up in a tree. And I was right. Not only could I see Jesus, but it turned out he could see *me*, too. He stopped right under the tree, looked up, and said, "Zacchaeus, come down immediately. I must stay at your house today." |
| MAN steps back in surprise. | **MAN**<br>He invited *himself*? |
| | **ZACCHAEUS**<br>Yup. And that really bothered some people because, besides being wee, I'm also a chief tax collector. I take money from people around here for taxes, and sometimes I used to take a little extra for myself. |
| MAN leans forward, interested. | **MAN**<br>Is that another reason you were up in a tree? So nobody could pick your pocket? |
| ZACCHAEUS wanders around CENTER STAGE a bit as he talks. | **ZACCHAEUS**<br>That did cross my mind. Anyway, Jesus came to my house, and I said, "Look, Lord. Here and now I give half of my |

possessions to the poor, and if I've cheated anybody, I'll pay back four times the amount." And you know what Jesus said?

**MAN**
Um, no.

**ZACCHAEUS**
He said, "Today salvation has come to this house, because this man, too, is a son of Abraham. For the Son of Man came to seek and save what was lost." And that was me—lost. Until I met Jesus!

**MAN**
So you're not cheating people anymore?

MAN shakes his head "no."

ZACCHAEUS tosses arms into the air in glad pronouncement.

**ZACCHAEUS**
Not one penny. I'm a changed man. When people ask me why, I say, "I just met Jesus."

**MAN**
That's great. So do you think maybe we should go over and tell those EMTs you're OK?

ZACCHAEUS puffs out his chest.

**ZACCHAEUS**
In the old days, I'd just let them keep chopping. Two more trees, and I won't need firewood for ten years. But now that I'm living for Jesus, I suppose we should say something...

**MAN**
Good idea.

MAN and ZACCHAEUS exit STAGE LEFT.

**EMT 2**
(Yelling from offstage) Timber!

**EMT 1**
(Muffled, a bit pained, sternly from offstage) Don't worry about me...I'm all right...Little help here...Someone... Anyone...Help!

## For Deeper Learning

Say: **When he met Jesus, Zacchaeus' life changed. He found that Jesus loved him, even though Jesus** *didn't* **love the cheating and lying Zacchaeus had been doing.**

**Jesus loves us, too. And just like Zacchaeus, there are things in our lives that Jesus wants to change.**

Have children form groups of three or four and discuss:

- **How do you think Zacchaeus felt when he found that Jesus loved him?**

- **What are things that changed in your life because of Jesus?**

- **What are things in your life that you think Jesus wants to change?**

# The Last Supper

**Bible Reference:** John 13:1-17

## Cast

JIM: adult male who is one of Jesus' disciples (James)

RUTH: adult female cleaning lady who's not afraid to talk to Jim

## Costuming: Jim wears a Bible-times costume and a cloak. Ruth wears a Bible-times costume.

## Props: Bible-times costumes, cloak for Jim

### SCRIPT

| ACTIONS | WORDS |
|---|---|
| *Play track 8 on CD B.* | |
| RUTH sticks her head in from STAGE LEFT. | **RUTH**<br>(Calling) Hello? The cleaning lady is here! Hello? Anyone here? |
| RUTH crosses to CENTER STAGE, looking around. | (To self) Boy, you'd think they'd at *least* clean off the table. You can always tell when all the guests at a meal were men. What a mess... |
| JIM enters from STAGE RIGHT. | **JIM**<br>Hi... |
| RUTH looks at JIM. | **RUTH**<br>(Embarrassed, flustered) Oh, I'm sorry! I didn't think anyone was here. Me and my big mouth... |
| JIM looks around. | **JIM**<br>That's OK. You're right; we *did* make a mess. |

**RUTH**

Are you gentlemen done with the meeting room? Have all your friends left?

JIM nods his head "yes."

**JIM**

Yeah, I just came back to pick up a cloak I left behind. The others are headed up to the Garden of Gethsemane. I have to catch up with them.

RUTH looks around the room.

**RUTH**

Did the room work for your meeting?

JIM nods his approval.

**JIM**

It was great. An upper room was just what we needed to celebrate the Passover together.

**RUTH**

I hope I'm not being nosy, but why the rush to leave? Most people finish their Passover meal and spend the evening telling stories about what God did in Egypt...

JIM shrugs his shoulders.

**JIM**

Well, you know Jesus—seems he's always going somewhere.

RUTH looks around to see if JESUS is still there.

**RUTH**

You mean Jesus the teacher? *He* was here?

JIM nods his head "yes."

**JIM**

Yup. You've heard of Jesus?

**RUTH**

(Awed) *Everyone's* heard about Jesus! He has made sick people better, brought dead people back to life...Some people say he's the Son of God.

**JIM**
They're right, but tonight Jesus was a servant.

**RUTH**
(Scoffing) Teachers like Jesus don't do the work of servants like me!

**JIM**
Actually, that's *exactly* what Jesus did. After the meal started and we were all seated, Jesus got up and poured water in a bowl. He took a towel and the water, and he started to wash our feet.

RUTH steps back a step or two.

**RUTH**
(Aghast) But that's a job only servants and slaves do! Teachers are too important to wash the feet of people like you...or me!

JIM closes the gap with RUTH.

**JIM**
That's what we thought. One of my friends, Peter, told Jesus he wasn't allowed to wash Peter's feet. But Jesus did it anyway.

**RUTH**
Why?

JIM moves DOWNSTAGE.

**JIM**
He was showing us that *everyone* should serve others. Jesus used himself as an example.

**RUTH**
Wow! So someone important like *you*—a friend of Jesus—should be willing to serve others?

**JIM**
Yup.

RUTH looks down.

**RUTH**
Even someone like *me*—a lowly cleaning lady?

JIM shakes his head "yes."

**JIM**
Yup.

**RUTH**
And your serving me would make Jesus happy?

JIM looks off, thoughtfully.

**JIM**
(Uncertainly) I guess so...

**RUTH**
(Brightly) Then you can help me clean up this mess. You start over there, and I'll start over here.

**JIM**
(Begrudgingly) Well, I guess Jesus *did* just show us how important it is to serve. We'll have to be quick so I can catch up with the rest of the disciples.

RUTH and JIM exit STAGE RIGHT as they clean.

**RUTH**
Great! Grab that towel over there. When we're done, maybe you can serve by cleaning my house.

## For Deeper Learning

Say: **Jesus served his followers, and we can serve others too!**

Have children form groups of three or four to discuss:

- **What's one way you serve others in your family or at school?**
- **Who is someone you think would be hard to serve? Why? How could Jesus use you to serve this person?**
- **In what ways has Jesus served you?**

# The Centurion and the Soldier

**Bible Reference:** Luke 23:44-49; John 19:16-30

## Cast

**ROMAN CENTURION:** adult male who is shell-shocked by what's just happened

**SOLDIER:** adult male who is a bit crude and calloused to the suffering he causes

**NARRATOR:** offstage voice who sets the stage

## Costuming:
The Roman Centurion wears a white Bible-times costume with a red tunic over it and carries a sword. The Soldier wears a Bible-times costume and carries a sword.

## Props:
Bible-times costumes, red tunic, 2 swords (You can make these by putting aluminum foil over cardboard.)

## Setup:
Before the play begins, you may want to drop the lighting in the room until the Narrator finishes speaking.

---

SCRIPT

| ACTIONS | WORDS |
|---|---|
| 💿 *Play track 9 on CD B.* | **NARRATOR**<br>They led Jesus out of the city, to the place called The Skull, where they crucified him along with two criminals—one on his right, the other on his left. The people stood watching, and the rulers sneered at him. The soldiers also came up and mocked him. There was a written notice above Jesus, which read: "This is the King of the Jews."<br><br>And about the sixth hour, darkness came over the whole land until the ninth hour. Jesus called out with a loud voice, "Father, into your hands I commit my |

spirit." And when he had said this, he breathed his last.

A centurion—a soldier who commanded one hundred men—saw what happened, praised God, and said, "Surely this was a righteous man."

ROMAN CENTURION enters STAGE RIGHT and slowly, dejectedly moves toward CENTER STAGE. SOLDIER enters STAGE LEFT and meets ROMAN CENTURION at CENTER STAGE.

## SOLDIER
(Amiably) So, Marcus, how was it today? Like always?

## ROMAN CENTURION
(Flatly) No, today was...different.

SOLDIER looks at CENTURION.

## SOLDIER
(Mildly surprised) Different how? We crucify criminals. We take criminals to the hill outside town and put them on crosses. How could things be different?

CENTURION drops his head.

## ROMAN CENTURION
(Soberly) Today we...we...

## SOLDIER
(Impatiently) We *what*? Hey, if something went wrong on your shift, I want to know about it before my men and I go out on the afternoon crucifixions. Did you run out of crosses or something?

CENTURION looks at audience.

## ROMAN CENTURION
Today we killed an innocent man. A good man. A *godly* man.

## SOLDIER
(Amused) They *all* say they're innocent—you know that! About the time they figure out what's going to happen, they'll say *anything* to go free!

**Skit Nineteen:**
The Centurion and the Soldier

| | |
|---|---|
| CENTURION looks back at SOLDIER. | **ROMAN CENTURION**<br>(Flatly) Not this one. He didn't beg or threaten. He just...he just let us kill him. |
| | **SOLDIER**<br>Who'd you crucify on your shift? Two thieves and that Jesus-prophet-preacher guy, right? Is *he* the one who got you all upset? |
| CENTURION still hanging his head. | **ROMAN CENTURION**<br>(Flatly) We hung a sign over his head that said, "The King of the Jews." |
| SOLDIER wags his head back and forth. | **SOLDIER**<br>(Chuckling) "The King of the Jews." That's a good one. Did he think he really *was* a king? |
| | **ROMAN CENTURION**<br>(Flatly) I was there. I saw his eyes. Jesus *was* a king, an *innocent* king. |
| SOLDIER moves closer. | **SOLDIER**<br>(Stage whisper) Quit *talking* like that! You want to get in trouble? We're *soldiers*. We don't crucify innocent people! Jesus was an enemy of the Empire! A troublemaker! And now he's dead, right? |
| CENTURION nods his head "yes." | **ROMAN CENTURION**<br>(Flatly) He's dead. We made sure. |
| | **SOLDIER**<br>(Satisfied) Then it's settled. Over and done with. We won't see *him* again. |
| | **ROMAN CENTURION**<br>I'm not so sure. |

Looks at CENTURION.

SOLDIER nods his head "yes."

SOLDIER moves toward STAGE RIGHT.

SOLDIER exits STAGE RIGHT. ROMAN CENTURION watches him go and then turns and heads toward STAGE LEFT.

ROMAN CENTURION slowly exits STAGE LEFT as music plays.

## SOLDIER
(Mocking) You *believe* all that stuff about Jesus coming back to life again?

## ROMAN CENTURION
I'm just saying I've helped crucify hundreds of people. It's my *job*. But this one was different. I met Jesus, and...and he was a righteous man. Do you understand what I'm saying?

## SOLDIER
(Impatiently) Yeah, you're saying you're getting soft. You're *losing* it. The job finally *got* to you. *That's* what you're saying!

Well, not *me*. I have two more crucifixions to do, and I'm not gonna let *your* getting all soft and weird stop me. Go home and get some sleep. You'll feel better in the morning. And take my word for it: Jesus couldn't have *possibly* been innocent.

## ROMAN CENTURION
(Five second pause, somberly—to self) Except he *was* innocent. I *know* it...

## For Deeper Learning

Say: **Sad, huh? Even one of the soldiers who helped kill Jesus knew in his heart that Jesus hadn't done anything wrong. He even knew that Jesus was God's Son.**

**It's important that you understand that the Romans didn't kill Jesus. Jesus could have stopped his crucifixion at any time, but he didn't. He let himself be killed so he could be our sacrifice for sin.**

Have children form groups of three or four and discuss:

- **How do you think Jesus felt when he let himself be nailed to a cross even though he was innocent?**

- **If someone did something like that for you, what would you do for that person?**

- **What does it mean to you that Jesus died on a cross to pay for your sins?**

# Mary Magdalene

**Bible Reference:** Luke 24:1-12

## Cast

**MARY MAGDALENE:** assertive and vibrant adult female

**PETER:** cautious and concerned adult male

**JOHN:** not terribly bright adult male

**NARRATOR:** offstage voice who sets the stage

## Costumes: All puppets wear Bible-times costumes.

## Props: Bible-times costumes

---

### SCRIPT

| ACTIONS | WORDS |
|---|---|
| 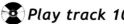 *Play track 10 on CD B.* | **NARRATOR**<br>On the first day of the week, very early in the morning, the women took the spices they had prepared and went to Jesus' tomb.<br><br>They found the stone rolled away from the tomb, but when they entered, they didn't find the body of Jesus.<br><br>While they were wondering about this, suddenly two men in clothes that gleamed like lightning stood beside them. The men said to them, "Why do you look for the living among the dead? He's not here; he has risen!"<br><br>So the women hurried away from the tomb and ran to tell Jesus' disciples.<br><br>**PETER**<br>**(From offstage)** I'll get it! |

| | |
|---|---|
| PETER enters STAGE LEFT and crosses to STAGE RIGHT. | **JOHN**<br>(Calling from offstage) If it's Roman guards here to kill us, don't let them in! |
| Calling STAGE LEFT. | **PETER**<br>I'll try to remember that!<br><br>(To self) Boy, he must think I'm as dense as a rock. |
| PETER pauses at edge of STAGE RIGHT. | (Calling) Who is it? |
| Muffled, through door; STAGE RIGHT channel. | **MARY MAGDALENE**<br>(From offstage) It's me—Mary Magdalene! Peter, let me in! |
| PETER exits STAGE RIGHT. | **PETER**<br>Mary? Hold on a minute... |
| PETER and MARY MAGDALENE enter STAGE RIGHT and cross to CENTER STAGE. | **MARY MAGDALENE**<br>(Out of breath) Boy, that door was *really* locked! |
| PETER looks at MARY. | **PETER**<br>Yeah, it's solid, all right. We don't want to take any chances. Ever since the Romans crucified Jesus, all of us disciples have been a little edgy. |
| | **JOHN**<br>(Calling from offstage) Peter, is it Roman soldiers here to kill us? |
| PETER looks STAGE LEFT. | **PETER**<br>(Calling) Relax, John! It's just Mary Magdalene! No soldiers! |
| MARY looks STAGE LEFT. | **JOHN**<br>(Calling from offstage) Hi, Mary! |

Skit Twenty:
Mary Magdalene

**VOICE 1**
How's it going, Mary?

**VOICE 2**
Thanks for coming by!

**VOICE 3**
Did she bring sandwiches or anything? I'm hungry!

PETER turns and looks at MARY.

**PETER**
(Concerned) You're so out of breath. Where have you been?

MARY is moving as if she is breathing hard.

**MARY MAGDALENE**
(Getting her breath) Out at the cemetery. We went to visit Jesus' grave.

PETER looks around as if someone might even be in the room already.

**PETER**
Are you sure that's smart? What if you were followed?

MARY stops the hard breathing and stands normally, looking at PETER.

**MARY MAGDALENE**
(Breathing normal now) That doesn't matter! Peter, he's not there! Jesus isn't there!

PETER draws closer to MARY.

**PETER**
(Confused) What do you mean?

MARY draws closer to PETER.

**MARY MAGDALENE**
(Excited) He's risen! He's risen from the dead!

PETER raises his hands in question.

**PETER**
(Baffled) What do you mean?

MARY raises both of her hands.

**MARY MAGDALENE**
(Growing impatient and shouting) I mean just what I said! *Jesus has risen from the dead!*

| | |
|---|---|
| OFFSTAGE LEFT. | **JOHN**<br>**(Calling from offstage)** What's she saying? Jesus was a friend of Fred? Who's Fred? Is he a Roman soldier come to get us? |
| PETER and MARY turn heads toward STAGE LEFT. | **PETER**<br>**(Calling)** John, no soldiers! It's OK! |
| OFFSTAGE LEFT. | **JOHN**<br>**(Calling)** Just checking! |
| MARY looks at PETER. | **MARY MAGDALENE**<br>I was with Mary, Jesus' mother. We went to the tomb, and the stone was rolled away from the entrance. |
| PETER looks toward audience. | **PETER**<br>**(Unbelieving)** Someone took Jesus' body? |
| | **MARY MAGDALENE**<br>That's what we thought at first, but there were angels, and they told us Jesus has risen from the dead. He's alive, Peter! Jesus is *alive*! |
| OFFSTAGE LEFT. | **VOICE ONE**<br>**(Calling from offstage)** What does Mary want? |
| PETER looks OFFSTAGE LEFT and raises hands to his mouth as if to yell. | **PETER**<br>**(Calling)** She's come from Jesus' tomb, and she says Jesus isn't there. He's risen from the dead! |
| OFFSTAGE LEFT. | **VOICE TWO**<br>**(Calling from offstage)** What is she, nuts? |
| OFFSTAGE LEFT. | **VOICE 3**<br>**(Calling from offstage)** Yeah, she's just excited! Of *course* he's there—the Romans *killed* him! |

**Skit Twenty:**
*Mary Magdalene*

136

| | JOHN |
|---|---|
| OFFSTAGE LEFT. | **(Calling from offstage; startled)** Romans? There are Romans here to kill us? |
| | **PETER**<br>**(Calling, aggravated)** John, get out from under the table! There are no Romans here! Repeat: *no Romans!* |
| PETER turns to MARY MAGDALENE. | John gets so scared... |
| MARY turns to PETER. | **MARY MAGDALENE**<br>**(Resolutely)** If you don't believe me, go see for yourself. I'm telling you, Jesus has risen from the dead, just like the angels told me! |
| | **PETER**<br>Well, I guess it couldn't hurt to look. If it's true, it changes everything... |
| MARY moves closer to PETER. | **MARY MAGDALENE**<br>**(Impatiently)** Peter, I just *met* Jesus! It's true, because *Jesus* changes everything! |
| PETER looks STAGE LEFT. | **PETER**<br>**(Calling)** Guys, I'm gonna go check this out. Who's coming with me? |
| JOHN steps onto stage from STAGE LEFT.<br><br>JOHN dashes across stage and exits STAGE RIGHT. | **JOHN**<br>**(Indignant)** I am, and I'll have you know that I am *not* scared. In fact, I'm going *first*, so don't even *try* to keep up! |
| | **PETER**<br>**(Urgently)** John, remember to open the...!<br><br>**(Calmly)** door. |
| MARY looks STAGE RIGHT. | **MARY MAGDALENE**<br>*That* had to hurt. |

MARY MAGDALENE and PETER hurriedly exit STAGE RIGHT.

**PETER**
He'll be OK. Come on! Let's go! If Jesus is alive, I want to know about it!

## For Deeper Learning

Say: **Jesus is alive! What a great message Mary heard and passed on to others! And it's as true today as it was thousands of years ago! We can pass along the same message, you know.**

Have children form groups of three or four and discuss:

- **How do you think Mary felt when she saw Jesus alive again? Why?**
- **If you'd been Peter, would you have believed Mary? Why or why not?**
- **Who's someone you could tell about Jesus being alive this week?**